# One Hundred Years of
# Roads and Rails
## AROUND THE SOLENT

' Si monumentum requiris, circumspice! '
' If you want a memorial, look around you! '

[Inscription in St. Paul's Cathedral in London]

# One Hundred Years of
# Roads and Rails
## AROUND THE SOLENT

David Fereday Glenn

Ensign
PUBLICATIONS

First published in 1991 by
**Ensign Publications**
a division of Hampshire Books Ltd.,
2 Redcar Street
Southampton SO1 5LL

**ISBN 1 85455 043 8**

Publisher : David Graves
Text files : Christine Pacey
Page make-up : The Precinct Press
Cover Design : Mark Smith
Printer : Printer Portuguesa, Lisbon

# CONTENTS

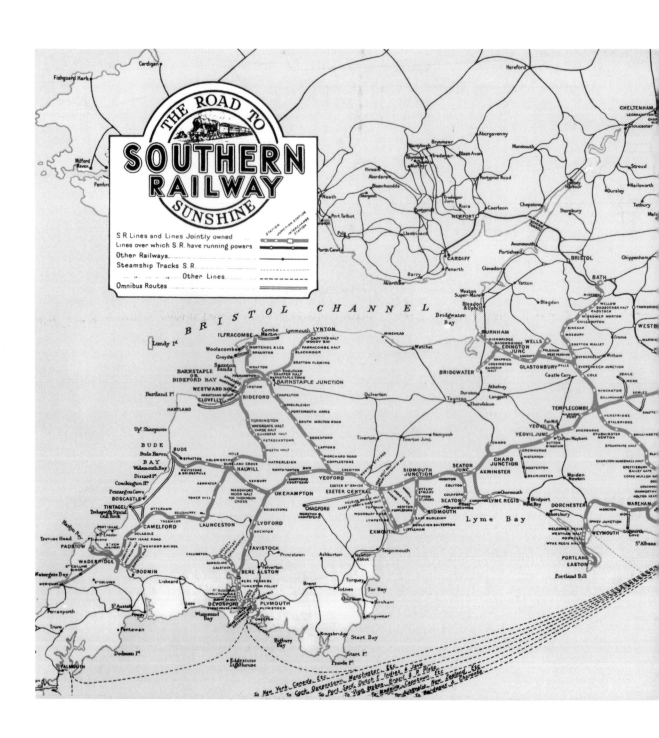

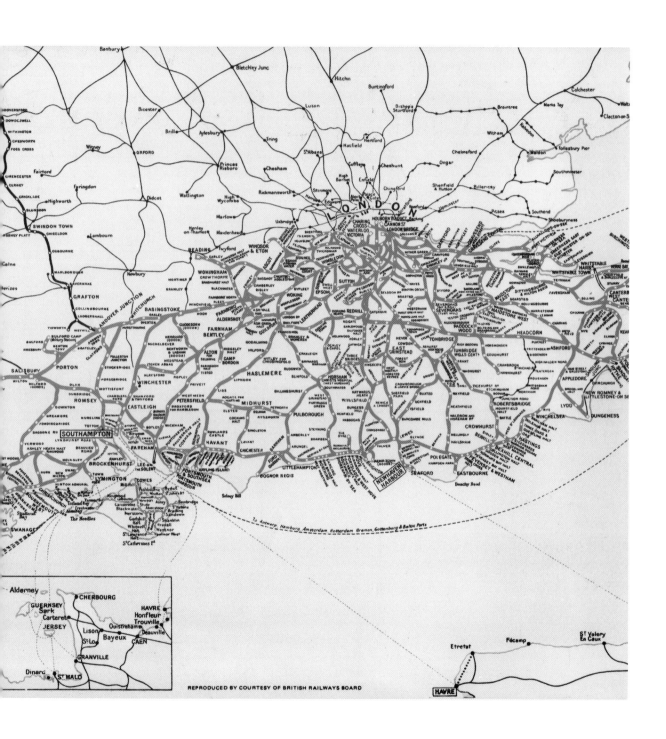

REPRODUCED BY COURTESY OF BRITISH RAILWAYS BOARD

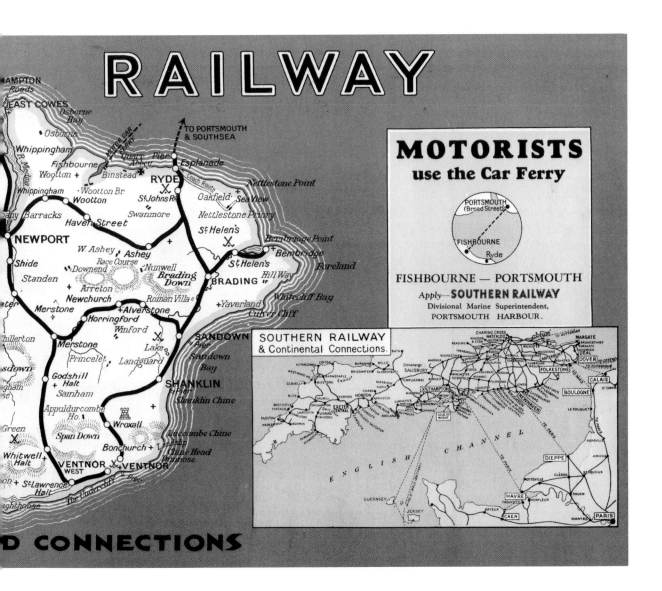

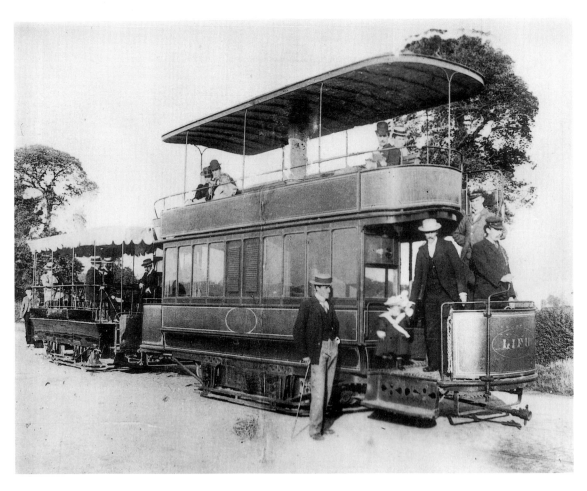

*Lifu was the steam tram built by the Liquid Fuel Engineering Company at Cowes in the Isle of Wight for the Provincial Tramways Company in Portsmouth during the final years before the system was taken over by the Corporation. This rural scene is at Landport. The gentleman standing on the front platform is believed to be John Fereday Glenn, who became Engineer and Manager of the Portsdown & Horndean Light Railway when it opened in 1903. (Mr. & Mrs. Leitch)*

# INTRODUCTION
## And Acknowledgements

Recently, a friend introduced me to an American visitor from Boston. He told me he was spending a semester teaching at St. John's College in Portsmouth. I told him I had been a pupil there from 1944 until 1948, and he wondered if any of the Brothers who had taught me then were still at the College. He suggested a few names and I reeled off some more. Much to my delight, it transpired that one or two I had known were now in retirement in Southsea, including Brother Maurice who had been my form teacher in the Upper Second and Lower Third!

What memories that conversation awoke! Like a benign Pandora's Box, recollections of childhood in the Forties came tumbling out: a season ticket that was only valid on Southdown buses (until 1946), queueing for up to an hour to get on a bus at Hilsea in the morning peak or being spoiled for choice at the Theatre Royal if one stayed late for choir practice in the evening. Despite the war and the rationing, the blackout and the 'doodlebugs', there was little sign of deprivation amid the bomb-damaged city and none at all of defeatism. Travelling might have been a crowded and sometimes difficult experience, but relief buses seemed to appear in droves and everyone got to their destination eventually. St. John's pupils' efforts to get to school on time could be reflected, in part, by the colour of the weekly 'testimonial', but I doubt if anyone suffered if he had a genuine excuse. And who would have thought, more than forty years on, that the motley assortment of public transport we used would still have any influence now? The fact that it does, dear reader, is the reason for writing this.

A decade ago I was thrilled to be commissioned to write a book about transport. Entitled *Roads, Rails & Ferries of the Solent Area, 1919 - 1969*, it was published in 1980. From the beginning it generated a good deal of interest, and I received letters from readers from many parts of the country and even different parts of the globe. That volume has now been out of print for a number of years but, as so much has occurred in the period since 1969 — the limit of its coverage — it is time to come back to the subject.

Some of the material unearthed for the original book could not be included for reasons of space, while fresh archive pictures have come to light within my own family. Lastly there has been a growing awareness throughout our society of the richness of our heritage, no less in transport than in anything else, as is witnessed by the number of vehicles and items of rolling stock being preserved and restored by private individuals in addition to the official museums. Every year there is a burgeoning calendar of anniversaries and events at which these treasures from the past can be displayed and inspected.

In this new volume the theme is still about transport — most especially public

During World War II the Ordnance Depot at the far end of Military Road at Hilsea was extended across Peronne Road. Sidings were installed to serve the extension, and the resident War Department shunting locomotive was a former Longmoor Military Railway 0-6-0ST, Woolmer'. It was built by Avonside Engineering of Bristol in 1910 and transferred to Hilsea in 1919; it is now preserved in the Museum of Army Transport at Beverley, Humberside.

Below : Southdown's Leyland Titan TD4 no. 123 (BUF 223), new in 1935, spent some years based at Hilsea after it was rebodied by East Lancs in 1946. In this view c. 1950 the bus is about to enter the garage after a rush-hour 45B duty from Fareham. (Surfleet)

transport — within striking distance of the Solent for the past 100 years. But whereas in my first book the sequence of events was chronological, here the treatment is by locality. Starting at Fareham, our journey around Hampshire is more or less in a clockwise direction, taking in the Isle of Wight, East Dorset and West Sussex on the way. From a rich assortment of pictures I hope readers may find much that is new. Particular mention should be made of the help given by *The News* of Portsmouth, whose present offices on the corner of Military Road at Hilsea are close to where I spent much of my childhood; in the Forties and Fifties, the older buses in the Southdown fleet used to be parked there overnight before the second garage at Hilsea West was constructed for them. Other photographers have also been most generous in allowing me access to their collections: Alan Cross, whose pictures of Hants & Dorset buses especially are a wonderful source of reference, and Alan Lambert with his formidable knowledge of Southdown and Hants & Sussex. There are others, too numerous to mention here, whose names appear with the captions for their photographs — I am grateful to them all. Any photographs not otherwise credited are from my own collection. I should also like to record my thanks to Margaret Lovell for help in proofreading and my son Miles for researching the maps.

It is only right that I should declare a special interest here, for the theme of transport has run through the veins of my family for more than a century. My great grandfather, John Glenn, and his brother Joseph Barber Glenn were active in promoting tramways long before electrification, not only in the Portsmouth area but also in other parts of the country. There is a horse tram preserved in Cardiff that bears the name of great-great uncle Joseph on its rocker panels, while the bodies of two early electric tramcars formerly operated by the Portsdown & Horndean Light Railway (another member of the Provincial Group) are now in the care of Portsmouth City Museums. How marvellous it would be if they could be restored, with grandfather's name (John Fereday Glenn) as Engineer and Manager, signwritten once more upon the flanks in time for their centenary in 2003! But, in the meantime, my elder son Miles and I — with help from a number of our friends in the Vintage Transport Association — have restored to active condition as mobile museum-pieces a trio of diesel buses from that *annus mirabilis*, 1949. Each in its different way represents a facet of my youth, when most motor buses had the engine and radiator at the front while the crew consisted of a conductor as well as a driver. In construction and technology they look back to the Thirties rather than forward to today, their simplicity and ruggedness based on the tried and tested formula of the pre-war era. By comparison with current designs they are short and narrow; a modern single-deck bus carries more passengers than a traditional double-decker from the Forties! But while we can smile at the quaintness of these antiquities, it is sobering to ponder how many of today's technological wonders will still be active after four decades, or more...

At first glance, the reader may be tempted to ask why this survey of transport starts at Fareham. Fareham does have a valid claim to fame in that the original part of its railway station was built in 1841 for the opening of the first branch line from Bishopstoke (now Eastleigh) through to Gosport. It also happens to have been my home since 1948, when my parents moved from Hilsea out into the country at Catisfield. Only 19 years before that, grandfather's emerald green tramcars of the Provincial (Gosport & Fareham) fleet were still terminating opposite the West End Inn just outside Fareham station! I suppose I must be firmly rooted in this part of Hampshire and, in any event, it makes a convenient starting point for this transport tour. Midway between Portsmouth and Southampton, clustered around the upper reaches of Portsmouth Harbour and washed by the tidal waters of the Wallington River, Fareham was a thriving market town of some 40,000 inhabitants; now it has grown out of all proportion and lost part of its charm. While the new shopping precinct may provide an essential focus for retail activity, the spaciousness of West Street has been needlessly sacrificed when it could have taken over the role of the bus station. Oxford, Exeter and Reading — to say nothing of certain other European cities — have somehow made public transport an integral part of shopping, to the benefit of all, whereas so much of the centre of Fareham has been laid waste for the mere parking of cars. Perhaps some of the photographs will serve to remind us how things used to be, not only in Fareham but all around the Solent.

*A horse-bus of the 1880s contrasts with a 1940s double-deck motor bus to mark the 115th Anniversary of the Mid-Hants Railway in 1980. The two are pictured at a rural crossroads in Ropley, whose station was opened in 1865, closed by British Rail in 1973 and re-opened as part of the preserved Watercress Line in 1977.*

# 1 · FAREHAM

## *Five Star Junction*

On 2 September, 1889, passengers and freight could travel, for the first time, direct by rail between Portsmouth and Southampton. While the railway had reached Southampton from London 50 years before that, a coastal link between these two important commercial centres was not a priority initially. Early sponsors favoured lines radiating outwards from the capital, for the most part, and it was not until later than more local considerations entered into the equation. From the Southampton end a branch was built from Portswood Junction (now St. Denys) curving sharply eastward to cross the River Itchen, then passing through Bitterne, Woolston and Sholing to terminate at Netley; it opened on 5 March, 1866. The main reason for its existence was the military hospital at Netley, for casualties of the Crimean War. Later on, a track was laid from Netley station directly into the hospital grounds so that the wounded could be brought in by train, as well as by launch, for the Royal Victoria Hospital had its own jetty, too. It took some time for the arguments in favour of extending the Netley branch another 73 miles to Fareham to win financial backing, for although only two stations at Bursledon and Swanwick were needed there was the Hamble River to be spanned by a girder bridge. In addition, there were other earthworks and some steep gradients to be surmounted, the line all the while twisting and turning to keep well above water level. It has never been an easy route to operate: steam haulage of all traffic lasted until 1957, thereafter the local

services went over to diesel multiple units leaving just freight and through trains in the hands of the idiosyncratic puffing monsters until their end came finally in mid-1967.

But if the Netley line was comparatively late upon the scene at Fareham, the Bishopstoke (Eastleigh) to Gosport branch was the first. Built with some difficulty in 1841, its opening on 29 November, proved rather premature as remedial work between Fareham and Botley had to be put in hand almost immediately! No centenary celebrations were possible because of World War II, and then the Fareham to Gosport section closed to passengers from 8 June, 1953. The line remained open for goods throughout until 1969, while a short section as far as Bedenham has managed to stay in use to the time of writing. As the Victorian Age drew to a close, nearly all the important rail arteries in Britain had been constructed, but territorial ambitions — real or imagined — sometimes led to speculative building of further routes. One such was the Meon Valley line between Fareham (Knowle Junction) and Alton (Butts Junction), opened in June, 1903. While provision was made during constructed for expansion to double track, this never proved necessary and the highly scenic route remained forever a rural backwater. However, its subsequent history could not be foreseen in 1903 and a new line from Knowle Junction to Fareham was authorised to minimise congestion through the Funtley tunnel. The new formation was built

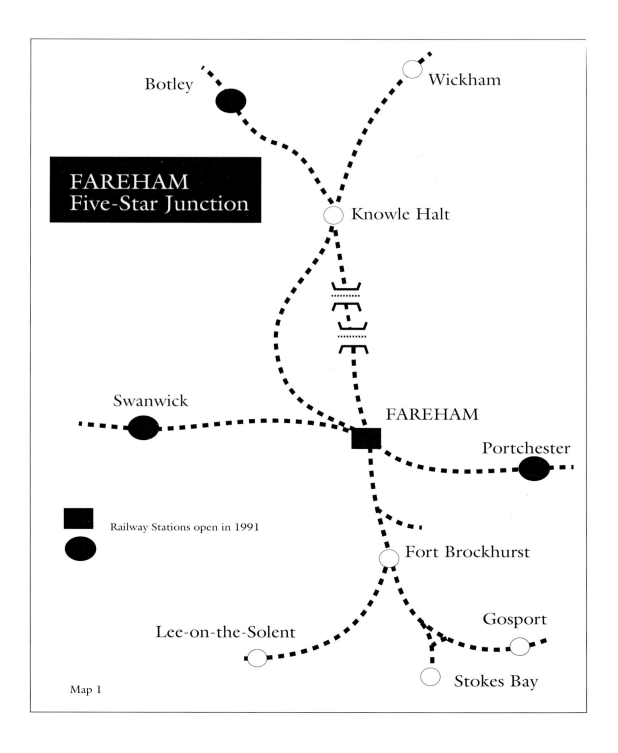

Map 1

for double track, which diverged to the west of the notorious tunnel just south of Knowle hospital. Gradients in either direction were quite severe, which meant in practice that heavy freight trains tended to be sent through the tunnel as before. This was to be the fifth point of the star of routes that characterised Fareham from the early 1900s.

The Gosport line, oldest and most prestigious, fathered two offspring during the 19th century. First, the branch to Stokes Bay was opened from 6 April, 1863, as a means of transferring passengers and luggage more easily to the Isle of Wight. Although it had some early success, once both London & South Western and London, Brighton & South Coast Railways had built their joint extension to Portsmouth Harbour in 1876, the Stokes Bay route faded; it closed from 1 November, 1915, although the tracks remained in place for some years afterwards. The most enduring feature, apart from the Pier, was the triangle of lines just outside Gosport station. That triangle was in almost daily use for turning steam locomotives until closure of the Meon Valley line from 7 February, 1955, but it was still there as late as 1959 when a steam-hauled special to commemorate the centenary of the Portsmouth Direct line (via Haslemere) ran through to Gosport. The Drummond 0-6-0 tender locomotive, 'Black Motor' Class 700 no. 30350 (built in 1897 by Dubs of Glasgow), reached Fareham from Guildford running chimney-first. It ran round its train and continued to Gosport tender-first. For the return journey, 30350 was turned on the triangle and then went back to Fareham still tender-first. As it traversed the same route heading home for Guildford and, ultimately, London, the elderly 'Black Motor' was able to revert to chimney-first operation once it had run-round again at Fareham. No doubt the crew appreciated the fact that tender-first working in the

very exposed cab of a late-Victorian locomotive was limited to the relatively slow passage in either direction of the four-and-a-half mile Gosport line on a cold January day!

From Fort Brockhurst - the only intermediate station between Fareham and Gosport — a further 'branch of a branch' was laid to Lee-on-the-Solent. Opening on 12 May, 1894, it began as a small independent concern operating from its own platform a little to the southwest of the LSWR station, using a contractor's locomotive at first. From 1909 the South Western provided a steam railcar to reduce running costs on the 3-mile line, but most examples of the type were withdrawn after a few years and Lee-on-the-Solent trains reverted to being loco-hauled. Nominally still independent at the Grouping, the little system was absorbed by the newly-created Southern Railway during 1923. It was an early casualty of harsh economics, with passenger traffic being withdrawn from 1 January, 1931, and freight at the end of October 1935. For some reason LBSCR designs seemed to find favour, for both the Brighton 'Terrier' (A1/A1x) 0-6-0T and the larger D1 0-4-2T classes appear in the relatively small number of photographs that are extant. Last train of all was worked by D1 0-4-4T no. 2239, now immortalised in a print in Gosport Museum.

So, by 1907 at the latest, Fareham had gained its '5-star' rating as a railway junction of some importance. The original route through to Gosport was still double-track, although the majority of passenger trains from both the Southampton and Eastleigh directions tended to terminate at Portsmouth. This trend was to accelerate first with singling of the Gosport line in 1933/4, except for a passing loop at Fort Brockhurst, then with travel restrictions imposed during World War II especially in an area deemed likely to be a military target.

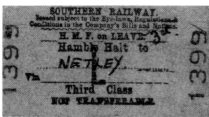

Between 1904 and 1907 the track layout between Fareham and Knowle Junction was revised and a new route avoiding the single bore tunnel installed to the west. This picture at Fareham station can be pinpointed to this period, thanks to the cross (signifying out of use) on the tunnel route arm of the signal gantry behind the engine. C8 no. 290 was the first of Dugald Drummond's early express 4-4-0s to be constructed for the LSWR in 1898, and appears to be at the head of a train for Netley and Southampton (T. Lawson)

The coal shortage of 1950 resulted in temporary loss of all passenger traffic, but when weekday services were resumed the writing was on the wall. By 1953 these had been reduced to a token operation of two each way, so withdrawal was inevitable. I travelled on the railway to and from Gosport just once, shortly before closure, the train consisting of an M7 0-4-4T and 3-coach LSWR non-corridor set. It was quite unremarkable at the time - one saw that kind of train on stopping services to Southampton Terminus, or to Eastleigh, Romsey and Andover Junction so regularly that it didn't even merit a photograph! Oh, the naivety of youth!

Such a cavalier disregard could perhaps be excused on the grounds that the line remained open for freight, and the loss of two passenger trains per day was no very big deal. It was a different story when closure of the Meon Valley was announced. Though I had never sampled the service throughout between Fareham and Alton, I spent many hours on the former station during school holidays and was often grateful for the existence of the branch train in bay platform 1. It would sit there patiently waiting for prospective travellers; the crew would fill the engine with water and rake out the ash from the smokebox to while away the time until departure, but at least it offered the spectacle of a live steam engine during the long pauses between more substantial action on the other lines. Two-coach trains were the norm, either push-pull with an M7 tank or a non-corridor set pulled by a tender engine. Only the first Down passenger train and the last Up service, latterly, warranted a tender engine; shedded at Guildford, the early morning arrival at Fareham continued light engine to Gosport, turned on the triangle, and came back at 11.45 in good time for the 12.23 pm pick-up goods along the valley to Alton. Likewise the engine off the 10.20 am freight

from Alton was due at Fareham at 3.34 pm, which allowed plenty of time for coaling, watering and turning on the Stokes Bay triangle before heading back up the valley with the 6.30 pm passenger train, the last one of the day. Drummond designs, either 4-4-0 or 0-6-0 machines, were regular performers in the 1950s; before that, Adams A12 'Jubilee' 0-4-2 tender engines had been commonplace since the turn of the century. In some parts of the country, and on certain other railways (or Regions in British Rail days), it was not normal practice to use large-wheeled four-coupled engines on freight — yet the Southern inherited no less than 80 mixed-traffic 4-4-0s of Drummond design in 1923 (the K10 and L11, small and large 'Hoppers', respectively) and found them well suited to the relatively modest pick-up goods duties that pertained on secondary and branch lines throughout the south and west. When the smaller-wheeled 4-4-0s went to the Valhalla in the sky around 1950/1, it was taken for granted that a pool of 'Greyhound' T9s and the last L12 4-4-0 (no. 30434) — each with massive 6'7" driving wheels — would soldier on with a little help from the even older Dubs-built Class 700 0-6-0s. And so it proved. But my chance to ride behind a 'Greyhound' along the Meon Valley branch did not occur until a couple of months after passenger services had been suspended.

On Thursday 14 April, 1955, I travelled with a couple of school friends in the brake van of the 12.23 pm pick-up goods from Fareham to Droxford and back. Powered by T9 4-4-0 no. 30732, the goods left Fareham's platform 1 with the engine running tender-first. There were two ex-SECR 'Dance Hall' brakes, one at either end of the train — we found from practical experience that fewer smuts were collected when travelling in the van furthest from the engine! It was eerie trundling through the twin Funtley tunnels in the darkness, smoke

*Southwards from Knowle Junction for about 1 mile three tracks ran parallel, consisting of the Up and Down lines avoiding Funtley tunnel between Fareham and Eastleigh (via Botley), while the third track served the Meon Valley branch and acted as a relief route for main line trains through the tunnel. On 6 June 1962, class U 2-6-0 no. 31808 heads a mid-day Andover Junction to Portsmouth service past Knowle Halt, this loco-hauled train doing its best to keep time as a replacement for a failed diesel multiple unit. Note the ground frame and siding for Knowle Hospital.*

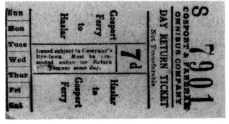

and steam from the old 'Greyhound' swirling about in the narrow bore, before emerging to pass the brickworks and abattoir sidings on the way to Knowle. The private siding and goods shed for the hospital were seldom used by this time and, like the two sidings at Funtley already mentioned, were only accessible for shunting with southbound trains. The single line 'tablet' issued by the signalman at Fareham East box, or Knowle Junction when heading south, could unlock the ground frames in each case so it was usual for traffic for any of these sidings to be delivered or collected by the Meon Valley goods, rather than by a main line freight train (for example, the 10.03 am Eastleigh to Fratton or the 11.27 am from Salisbury to Chichester). Tablets were exchanged at Knowle Junction box and again at Wickham, for as yet both trackwork and signalling remained just as they had for passenger trains; later, Wickham box would be closed and the track removed from the Down platform, but for now the only change was severance of the line just north of Droxford and no other train to pass.

On arrival at Wickham we stepped down from the brake van and watched the T9 shunting in the yard. There was a ramshackle old goods shed astride one of the sidings, a feature shared only with Farringdon along the whole length of the Meon Valley. Giving a piercing blast on its whistle, 30732 drew a string of wagons out of the yard and slowly shunted them back into the Up platform to reform the train. Being only a pick-up goods, all wagons were loose-coupled without continuous brakes, so there was a fair amount of clanging and banging from buffers and brake gear during this process. Once that was completed, we clambered back on board and awaited departure. One advantage of the 'Dance Hall' type of brake van is that it has a large canopied verandah at both ends, and we were able to

enjoy the view forward as well as behind us while the rural freight wound its way along.

Beyond Wickham the track passed through the lovely Forest of Bere; fresh green shoots were sprouting everywhere, and no 1st class ticket on the most important express could have been more worthwhile than that ride in a humble goods train. The width of the occasional road overbridge confirmed the original scheme to double the track if traffic had expanded sufficiently. At the approach to Droxford the gradient steepened and a long siding appeared on the western side — this proved to be the goods yard headshunt — and the journey was almost over. The signalbox on the Up platform was still in use as we drew to a stand, and the locomotive was uncoupled ready to carry out its routine shunting duties. These were soon concluded, and 30732 attached itself to the southern end of the train, chimney first. There was plenty of time of explore, and even buy a drink at the Railway Inn on the corner of Hambledon Road outside the station — the hostelry is now known as The Hurdles since the railway is no more!

By 2.45 pm the return goods was ready to depart. There was no starting signal southbound from the Up side, but the signalman raised the inner home that he had pulled off when the train had approached from Fareham, just to show the line was clear. The ride back was over all too soon, for there was no shunting to do at Mislingford goods, while at Wickham there was only a brief pause just to exchange tablets. With the old 'Greyhound' running freely, it was quite a lively trip in the rear brake van to Knowle Junction. The tablet was exchanged for the last time before the train plunged into the intense darkness of the two consecutive tunnels at Funtley.

Buffers clanged as the locomotive brakes

A Salisbury to Portsmouth van train hauled by Standard 4MT 4-6-0 no. 75079 accelerates through Bursledon in readiness for the steep ascent to Swanwick on 25 May 1961. Some years later the station buildings were demolished and the platforms lit by fluorescent tubes, but in this view gas lamps are still in use.

Left : The afternoon train from Reading General to Portsmouth & Southsea sometimes produced a Remembrance class 4-6-0 — these seven engines had been built as 4-6-4Ts for the LBSCR but rebuilt in the mid-1930s when the Brighton line was electrified, ending their days at Basingstoke shed (70D). On 13 April 1955, class N15x no. 32327 Trevithick was rostered for the 1.48 pm from Reading, pausing briefly at Botley on route for Portsmouth.

were applied for the approach to Fareham - we were early and the home signal remained obdurately in the horizontal position for some minutes. Then, with a bit of a 'snatch', the goods moved forward to surrender the tablet at East box before running into platform 1. We said our goodbyes and jumped down, the round trip of 18 miles or so completed — in another seven years, almost to the day, there would be more farewells when the very last official freight ran to Droxford...

Outside Fareham station, a passenger arriving by train in the early 1900s would walk along the comparatively short 'carriage drive' past the Railway Hotel down to the main Southampton to Portsmouth road. An electric tramway had been built in 1905 from a simple terminal at the road junction opposite the West End Inn through the centre of Fareham and on to Gosport. As Provincial Tramways had operated one of their subsidiaries on the other side of the Harbour under the name of the Portsmouth Street Tramways Company — until municipalisation in 1901 — their system from Fareham was shown on the tramcars themselves as the Gosport & Fareham Tramways. There had been an earlier horse-drawn tramway in Gosport itself from 1882, but a narrower track was used and the whole thing had to be relaid to 'standard' gauge with the coming of the electric cars. Yet, after only a quarter of a century, the modern system was abandoned and replaced by a fleet of rather modest Chevrolet single-deck buses. With the benefit of hindsight, it has to be said that this was an unfortunate decision — even if it was provoked by objections to the Provincial plan to link up both Gosport & Fareham and the similar Portsdown & Horndean Light Railway with a line through Portchester. The London & South Western Railway, which had already experienced the effects of competition from urban tramcars in Portsmouth and

Southampton, blocked the tramway's logical development on the ground that it would threaten the railway's traffic between Fareham and Portsmouth. This might have been overstated to make the argument more convincing, but the railway did have a point! On the other hand, whilst there might have been some loss of local traffic, many of the trains between Fareham and Portsmouth commenced their journeys from much further afield — from Salisbury (or beyond), from Andover Junction or (since 1889) from Southampton. Whatever the rights and wrongs of the argument, the railway succeeded in maintaining its monopoly from Fareham to Cosham and buses replaced tramways of all kinds by the end of 1936 — not only the Gosport & Fareham trams, but the Portsdown & Horndean Light Railway cars and even those of Portsmouth Corporation, too. The only urban system to remain anywhere in the Solent area after that date was in Southampton, which we shall come to later.

As well as its importance as a railway junction, Fareham has also been a major interchange for those travelling by bus. Boundaries before the Road Traffic Act of 1930 tended to be somewhat blurred, with individual operators testing the market and competing with each other in rather haphazard fashion. For example, during the 1920s it was possible to travel by Southdown bus from Portsmouth to Southampton or Winchester, while a similar journey could be undertaken in a Hants & Dorset vehicle. These two companies were happy to co-operate with each other if it meant that a smaller rival could be squeezed out — as occurred when Fuger tried to provide a through service from Warsash to Portsmouth in 1929/30. When the dust settled it was decided to build a joint bus station on the corner of Portland Street at its junction with West Street in Fareham, with facilities for both Southdown

( Continued on page 29 )

The morning train on weekdays from Reading General to Portsmouth was frequently the best opportunity to see a former Great Western locomotive at work. On 15 March 1958, 4-6-0 no. 4998 Eyton Hall with a 3-coach Bulleid 'shortie' set is seen coasting into Fareham from the double track avoiding route at 11.10 am — since 1972 these lines have been lifted and houses have filled the empty space as far as Highlands Road; all services between Eastleigh and Fareham now use the single-bore Funtley tunnel instead.

The nerve centre of most railway operations was the signal box. Where there were two, they were distinguished according to their location — thus the larger box (pictured centre) was Fareham East, on the east side of the main line, while the other, Fareham West was located on the opposite side at the southern end of the station. Note the single line tablet in its pouch for the next train to Eastleigh via Funtley tunnel and Knowle Halt.

Drummond Black Motor 0-6-0 no. 30350 slows for the level crossing at Fort Brockhurst station on the Gosport line with the Portsmouth Direct Line Centenarian special on 25 January, 1959. To the left of is the Admiralty siding and overgrown platform; the branch to Lee-on-the-Solent diverged from the main line south of the station, in former times. Ordinary passenger traffic to Gosport ceased from 8 June 1953, freight continued until January 1969.

*Lee-on-the-Solent, a popular desti-
nation for Bank Holiday crowds.
The Pier Hotel was opposite the
railway terminus, but the long queue
for Hants & Dorset buses suggests
the picture was taken after closure
in 1931. The open-top bus appears
to be one of Hants & Dorset's first
double-deckers, a Leyland GH7.
New in 1926, they soon became ob-
solete after introduction of the Titan
TD1 in 1928. Shifting holiday-
makers was one of its final tasks for
the company.*

*Its spell of shunting over, class U 2-
6-0 no. 31808 prepares to leave
Gosport with the lunchtime goods
on 28 March, 1962. The 1841-built
terminus was damaged during
World War II, after which a metal
train-shed was substituted for the
original timber structure; in the
background on the right can be seen
the remains of the classic station
designed by Sir William Tite. A
single track continued beyond
Gosport station, across Spring
Garden Lane and Mumby Road,
into Clarence Yard for the RN base.*

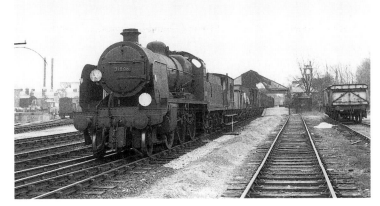

*A reminder of how Gosport junction at Fareham
used to look: on 27 June, 1955, one of the Brighton-
constructed 4MT 2-6-4T locomotives designed
by Fairburn for the LMS is taking water at the
southern end of platform 2. Although officially
allocated to Bricklayers Arms depot (73B), a few
examples of this type could be found working on
local passenger duties around Eastleigh (71A)
until 1957. The lower-quadrant signal arms on
the gantry had smaller repeaters at eye level for
the benefit of drivers of stopping trains; upper
quadrants were fitted in 1956.*

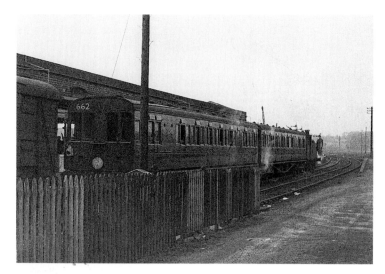

*Platform 1 at Fareham, with the 1.30 pm from Alton on 29 January, 1955. Class M7 0-4-4T no. 30054 and former SECR push-pull set 662 would form the 2.48 pm departure for the Meon Valley branch after the engine has been serviced and taken water from the column at the end of the platform. By 1990 these tracks no longer existed and the former goods yard has, for the most part, been converted as a car park for commuters.*

*The unique 4-cylinder exhaust beat of a Lord Nelson class 4-6-0 (no. 30857 'Lord Howe') echoes around the cutting where the original 1841 route meets the double-track deviation of 1906/7 almost two miles north of Fareham. On 27 February, 1962, Lord Howe was employed on the 11.08 am Fratton Yard to Eastleigh ECS train, diverted via Funtley tunnel owing to a landslip on the avoiding lines that caused one track to be taken out of use. Since 1972/3 all trains have used the single line through the tunnel.*

*Wickham station, with the Up goods during shunting operations on 14 April, 1955. Although passenger services on the Meon Valley line were discontinued from 7 February, no changes have yet been made to trackwork or buildings: the shelter on the Down platform is still in situ and the signal box remains in use. Class T9 4-4-0 no. 30732 is engaged in shunting the yard.*

*With Knowle Hospital on the skyline, class Q1 0-6-0 no. 33039 brings the nine-coach Eastleigh Works special (5.20 pm Eastleigh to Fratton service on weekdays only) past Funtley abattoir siding on 21 August, 1962. Since May 1990 this route has been electrified, the siding long since removed.*

*Contrasts at Fareham on 7 July, 1955 — in platform 3 the handsome lines of 4-6-0 no. 4993 Dalton Hall grace the 2.45 pm from Portsmouth & Southsea to Reading General while beyond, in platform 1, Drummond Greyhound 4-4-0 no. 30300 pauses between shunting operations, having arrived back at Fareham shortly before with the Meon Valley goods from Droxford. Note the LSWR water crane on the left and the old non-corridor carriages (also LSWR) behind the Western Region locomotive on the right.*

From September 1949 Southdown Motor Services extended the infrequent 35 service to and from Fareham railway station. For just a couple of years it continued to run to Chalton or Petersfield before being cut back — first to Droxford and Hambledon, then to Southwick only. This rare picture shows 1454, a Harrington-bodied Leyland 'Tiger' TS8, outside the Railway Hotel at Fareham in 1950 or 1951 waiting to depart to Chalton on either a Thursday or a Saturday afternoon. The single fare was 1/11d (10p). (A.Lambert)

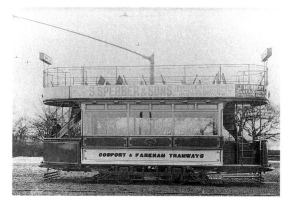

Portchester station is perched on an embankment mid-way between Fareham and Cosham on the former LSWR line constructed in 1848. It provides the setting for class D1 4-4-0 no. 31735 and a single parcels van on the morning of 14 July, 1959, on their way to Portsmouth. Gas lamps were still in vogue, along with semaphore signals, while two-coach diesel trains maintained local passenger services.

New in 1906 in readiness for the electrification of the second route from Gosport to Bury Cross, tram-car no. 16 was posed for the camera at Hoeford depot of the Provincial Tramways Company. Seating fifty-five, this car was built by Brush and mounted on a Brill 21E truck. On the lower right-hand corner of the rocker panels appeared my grandfather's name: J. Fereday Glenn, Manager. The garter around the fleet number is still a feature of People's Provincial buses.

and Hants & Dorset services. The latter garaged its buses there also, while Southdown maintained a small 'dormy' shed at Warsash and built a modest depot close to the Railway Hotel, by Fareham station. With the exception of the Fareham to Warsash route, which remained jointly operated by these two main bus companies for the best part of half a century, Fareham became the natural boundary between Southdown and Hants & Dorset; it was also the meeting point with Provincial's Gosport & Fareham services, as well as several independents. Provincial gradually acquired the stage carriage services of all the smaller operators in the Gosport area — the last in May 1953 — and then took over the former Millard route between Fareham and Catisfield from Hants & Sussex in December 1954; Smith's bus route to Funtley and Knowle was absorbed two months later.

Hants & Sussex had brought the 'big fleet' image to the Catisfield route in 1946. No one could fail to spot the red double-decker parked outside the old fire station in West Street at Fareham. By 1948 it was generally a Leyland 'Titan' PD1 with Northern Coachbuilders bodywork on service 14; alternate journeys ran only to Highlands Road Corner (the junction with Kiln Road), the outward route being via West Street, Trinity Street, Park Lane and Kiln Road. I found it a useful alternative route to Catisfield village, especially if I had just missed the through Southdown 45 bus to Warsash (one per hour) or the corresponding Hants & Dorset 77. A double-deck PD1 — the first Leyland design for the postwar years — was not commonly to be found at Fareham on either the Southdown or Hants & Dorset operations before the 1950s, although both fleets had such vehicles in use, so the Hants & Sussex bus was quite avant-garde.

There was the added attraction of genuine Bell-punch type tickets being issued instead of the paper T.I.M. variety popularised by both Southdown and Provincial; Hants & Dorset still had Bell-punch tickets on some routes (notably the 80 to Woolston) but they were a vanishing phenomenon. If my memory serves me right, the red bus left Fareham Market at half-past the hour on Catisfield journeys, running past the main Bus Station before turning north into Trinity Street opposite the church. The PD1 was fitted with the 7.4 litre oil engine that Leyland developed for many of its lorries during the war, being very economical but not fast-revving, so much of the ascent past Price's School had to be in 3rd gear until the summit at North Hill. Kiln Road was flat, then followed the undulating Highlands Road to Hill Park Stores. As there was no direct access on to the A27 road then, the bus continued along Highlands Road until it met the lane that came up from Catisfield Fork (now Peak Lane crossroads) and turned right into the village itself. After unloading opposite the little 'tin' church of St. Columba's, the bus reversed in front of Catisfield Post Office in readiness for the return journey. This was the same only as far as North Hill, after which the 14 service descended Old Turnpike, where it met up with the A32 Wickham Road, coming back into Fareham by way of High Street so that it was facing the right way ready for the next trip when it pulled up in front of the fire station.

Some readers may wonder how the inhabitants of the upper part of Trinity Street and Park Lane got back into Fareham, as the Hants & Sussex bus travelled only in a northerly direction between West Street and North Hill: until Provincial took over the service, the chances are they were obliged to use shanks' pony! By 1955, when Provincial had absorbed both the Catisfield service and Smith's route to

Fareham bus station in the 1930s and 1940s: the west side was the domain of Hants & Dorset, while Southdown routes to Portchester, Cosham and Portsmouth used the east side. It had a small servicing bay and could garage a dozen or so Hants & Dorset vehicles. Inside can be seen Leyland Lion LT5A BA102 (ALJ 784) and a double-deck Bristol K5G, while outside Beadle-bodied Bristol L5G TS664 (BOW 163) prepares to leave for Burridge. (Hants & Dorset coll.)

Southdown and Portsmouth Corporation established a co-ordination agreement on 1 July, 1946, within an area bounded by Emsworth, Petersfield and Fareham. This resulted in sporadic appearances of crimson Corporation buses at Fareham bus station. This was most pronounced during 1948, when Wadham-bodied Leyland Cheetah no. 43 (BTP 943) appeared on the 138 service to Cosham via Portsdown Hill. (J.E. Cull)

Hutfields of Gosport acquired several lowbridge Leyland Titan double-deckers from Southdown in the late-1950s. A pair of Beadle-bodied TD5s (nos. 192/6, EUF 192/6) became a familiar sight in the area, repainted in a smart red and cream livery, on school contracts, football specials to Fratton Park and late-night transport from Southsea's clubland on Saturdays. Pictured when Portland Street was still in use for two-way traffic, lowbridge 192 prepares to turn into Fareham's West Street closely followed by an East Lancs-bodied TD4 (125: BUF 225) of Southdown. (Surfleet)

*Fareham's West Street in the late-1950s, with a representative choice of popular family cars heading east on the A27 — there were no traffic lights in the town, then. Southdown was using a 1939 Leyland Titan TD5 on the 45A service via Castle Street (Portchester) — no. 244 (GCD 44) had a 1949 East Lancs body fitted, modified with 3-track route numbers in case of need. The A32 to Gosport squeezed into Quay Street on the right, beside the Bugle Hotel. (The News, Portsmouth)*

Knowle hospital, via Funtley, some rationalisation was possible. The 'short' journeys that had formerly terminated at Highlands Road Corner were extended alternatively to Fareham Park Estate and the new Heathfield Estate. With a 20-minute headway and two buses, it was possible to serve all three destinations (Catisfield, Fareham Park and Heathfield) once hourly for much of the day.

The Knowle route could be worked by a solitary single-decker most of the time, with additional journeys being provided on Thursdays and Sundays to cater for hospital visiting times. The former Hants & Sussex service was renumbered 17 (no matter which destination) and the Knowle route became 18 in the Provincial timetable. The 17 service continued to use the fire station bus stop outside Fareham

As Mr. Orme White, manager at Provincial for many years, lived in Kiln Road, he liked to see a new or freshly-painted bus on the Hill Park routes. Drawn up at the stop in West Street outside the Fire Station and Melgrade Cafe in 1958 was the full-fronted no. 70 (SCG 622), one of only two Guy Arab IV models bought new that year, that dominated the 17 service until the first Deutz air-cooled creation emerged from Hoeford. (D. Clark)

A late-Fifties scene at Hoeford garage. The much-rebuilt AEC Regal on the left (no. 29: CG 9608) joined the fleet in 1934 and was adapted for one-man operation in 1957 — the last example of this type did not retire until 1970, being retained for the Fareham to Knowle (18) service. The Park Royal-bodied Guy Arab kept its utility appearance throughout a long career with Provincial — new in 1943, no. 56 (EHO 868) was converted to open-top in 1955. (R.E. Mack)

Market, as before, with the inward journeys returning via Old Turnpike and High Street just as in Hants & Sussex days. However, the Knowle service departed from outside Kimbells' shop on the opposite side of West Street, travelling via High Street, Old Turnpike, Kiln Road and Funtley, returning from North Hill via Park Lane and Trinity Street —

thus, at last, catering for passengers in either direction! The single-decker to Knowle was an elderly AEC 'Regal' adapted for one-man operation, while the double-deck bus on route 17 was usually a newly-rebodied or repainted vehicle, perhaps because it passed the home of Provincial's Managing Director, Mr Orme White...

*One day each year it was the custom to close Wickham Square to all traffic to hold the fair. This evocative picture recalls the great days of steam gallopers (roundabouts), while some of the showmen's caravans on the left appear to be former Aldershot & District single-deck Dennis buses — OT 8900, with oval rear window, is nearest to the photographer. The low, flat-roofed building near the King's Head Hotel may be a wartime shelter for local residents, so the scene may date from 1946. (The News, Portsmouth)*

*Before the days of Hampshire diesel units, the Sundays only 1.23 pm from Eastleigh to Portsmouth was hauled by steam and called at Knowle Halt for the benefit of visitors to the hospital. On 6 January, 1957, 4MT 2-6-0 no. 76007 was in charge, coasting out of Funtley tunnel along the single track towards Fareham with Bulleid corridor set no. 859. Note the traditional timber-bodied wagons in the goods yard head-shunt.*

With only months to go before the end of steam traction, Battle of Britain 4-6-2 no. 34090 (formerly named *Sir Eustace Missenden, Southern Railway*) looks in woebegone condition as it tackles the 1 in 100 adverse gradient 'wrong line' from Fareham with the Fratton to Eastleigh ECS train on 6 February, 1967. The erstwhile Down line of the deviation between Knowle and Fareham had to be used by Up trains owing to the landslip beyond Highlands Road bridge.

Through trains between Plymouth and Brighton usually conveyed a portion for Portsmouth as far as Fareham. On 29 April, 1955, when the main train from Plymouth left Fareham for Brighton behind the inevitable Bulleid West Country 4-6-2, the remaining four coaches for Portsmouth were left behind in platform 2. Class C2x 0-6-0 no. 32549 was summoned from the Gosport line, to take over for the 10-mile run to Portsmouth & Southsea (Low Level).

# 2 · SOUTHAMPTON WATER
## *And its Environs*

Sir Winston Churchill once remarked that he was 'a child of the House of Commons'. In like fashion perhaps it could be said that I am a child of the two Solent cities, since my father was born in Portsmouth and my mother in Southampton (I myself was born in Southsea, Portsmouth). Certainly, such family associations could go a long way towards explaining my abiding interest in transport all around the area! My earliest conscious experience of Southampton occurred in August 1944: the D-Day landings had taken place only two months before and World War II was reaching a decisive phase. The family had just been for the first holiday away since hostilities began, and we were on board the train from Exeter returning to Portsmouth when there was an air-raid warning. The train seemed to stay in the platform at Southampton Central station for a long time and, while waiting for it to continue, I amused myself with looking out of the window. In the distance I could just make out the upper decks of trams and buses going about their business — it must have been the first time I had ever seen trams in my life.

Horse trams had begun operating in Southampton as early as 1879 and the system was taken over by the Corporation in 1898; electrification started in 1900. An experimental motor bus service was tried the following year, but it was not considered to be a success and was abandoned after a few months. Not until 1919 was the experiment tried again! But even with the coming of regular motor buses, the advance of the tramway continued unabated until 1930, when the line from Bassett crossroads to Swaythling was inaugurated. Only two sections of tram route were taken out of use before World War II, and one of those remained serviceable for workmen's cars; special sidings were constructed during the war away from likely enemy targets to aid dispersal of the fleet, particularly at night. But once hostilities ceased and deliveries of new motor buses began to arrive, the end was in sight for the last tramway system in the south (excluding London, which lingered on until 1952). Closure came in stages during 1948/9, with the last public services taking place on 31 December, 1949; no. 9 was specially decorated for the occasion, being one of the domed-top cars always associated with manager Percy Baker and the Bargate routes. One of the original open-top cars with knifeboard seating, also designed for the Bargate, was sold to a group of enthusiasts and can now be seen beautifully restored to full working order at the Tramway Museum at Crich in Derbyshire, while other car bodies have since been recovered and are undergoing renovation locally.

It was not until the 1930s that motor-buses began to make very much of an impact on Southampton. From 1919 there had been the solid-tyred open-top Thornycroft 'J' models, but the state of the roads did not mean instant popularity for the internal combustion-engined machines. A batch of huge three-axled covered-top buses with pneumatic tyres

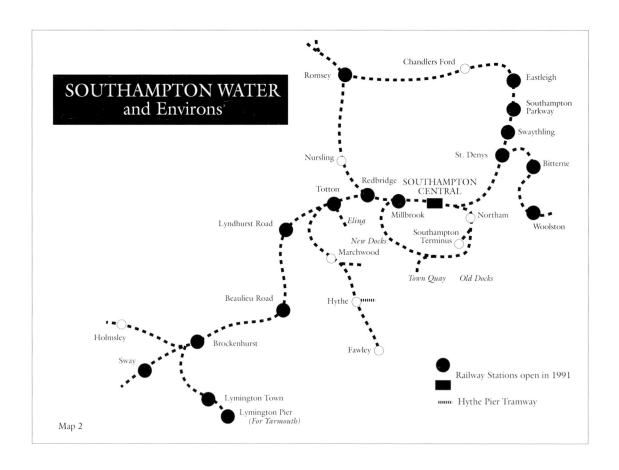

## SOUTHAMPTON WATER and Environs

Chandlers Ford

Romsey

Eastleigh

Southampton Parkway

Swaythling

Nursling

St. Denys

Bitterne

Redbridge   SOUTHAMPTON CENTRAL

Totton

*Eling*

Millbrook

Northam

Lyndhurst Road

Woolston

*New Docks*

Southampton Terminus

Marchwood

*Town Quay*     *Old Docks*

Beaulieu Road

Hythe

Holmsley

Sway

Brockenhurst

Fawley

● Railway Stations open in 1991

■

▪▪▪ Hythe Pier Tramway

Lymington Town

Lymington Pier
*(For Yarmouth)*

Map 2

G.W.R.
_____

Northam

L. & S. W. R.

0084

SOUTHERN RAILWAY.
This Ticket is issued subject to the By-laws
Regulations & Conditions stated in the
Company's Time Tables Bills & Notices
Available on DAY of issue ONLY.
MARCHWOOD   TO
*Hythe Hants*
Via
1st Class. Fare 10d

0084

5115

7 | 8 | 9 | 10 | 11 | 12

British Transport Commission   (S)

LYNDHURST ROAD
PLATFORM TICKET 2d.

Available one hour on day of issue only
Not valid in trains. Not transferable
To be given up when leaving platform.
For conditions see over

1 | 2 | 3 | 4 | 5 | 6

5115

appeared at the end of the Twenties, but they were not noted for their success either! Some of the early buses were painted in the tramway livery of crimson and cream, but later standard designs — such as the AEC 'Regent', Guy 'Arab' and Thornycroft 'Daring' double-deckers as well as most of the little Leyland 'Cub' single-deck buses — were delivered in an attractive livery of blue and ivory. With the coming of wartime austerity all light coloured paintwork became grey, and subsequent deliveries and repaints standardised on the tramcar colours. While there have been inevitable variations in the intervening years, today's City Bus livery represents a logical development from the colours used on generations of tramcars (as represented by knifeboard car no. 45 at Crich). Experiments with diesel-engined buses in the Thirties proved successful and resulted in standardisation, throughout the 1940s and 1950s, on the Gardner-engined Guy 'Arab' model for all double-decks and most single-deckers, too. The only exception was a trio of little Albion 'Nimbus' saloons for the Swaythling local service to Allington Lane or South Stoneham Cemetery (route 10), purchased in the late 1950s. These vehicles were required to negotiate the low railway arch which, incredibly, straddled the cross-country trunk road — the A27 — until the motorway relieved that acute bottleneck in the 1980s.

Southampton Corporation's last traditional buses were purchased in the period from 1960-68, but there was much less standardisation than before. Two series of Leyland 'Titan' PD2 double-deckers allowed some of the older Guys to be withdrawn, but most of them were resold to other operators including Provincial (Gosport & Fareham), where they continued to give honourable service and add to their already vast mileage. But the bulk of new acquisitions came from AEC, whose 'Regent' V model dominated the local scene until 'one-

person' operation on all routes compelled their retirement; bodywork was by Park Royal, East Lancs and Neepsend, the final examples having semi-automatic gearboxes. Then a new standard was set with the coming of the rear-engined Leyland 'Atlantean' in large numbers from 1968 onwards.

As well as running trams and motor buses, the Corporation on 29 September, 1934, took over management of the Floating Bridges across the River Itchen at Woolston. The Floating Bridge had been launched by a private company on 23 November, 1836, as an alternative to the high tolls once charged for use of the road bridge at Northam. Just as Netley Hospital provided the incentive to build a branch railway from Portswood (St. Denys) so the hesitant beginnings of the chain-driven Floating Bridge were boosted by the extra traffic to and from the Woolston side of the river, requiring a second Bridge to be in operation by 1881. With a third kept in reserve for emergencies, routine maintenance etc., the Corporation inherited Bridges 8, 9 and 10 (all being steam driven), while those diesels that replaced them lasted until the new high-level road bridge was opened in May 1977 (numbers 11, 12 and 14; a superstitious Council avoided the use of 13!). Foot passengers were allowed to travel free from 30 September, 1946. Often during the 1960s and 1970s I preferred to drive my car to Southampton using the quieter road from Lowford (Bursledon) through Sholing to Woolston, then savour a few minutes' relaxation as the Floating Bridge clanked across the Itchen, before driving off on the opposite shore round past the Docks. It was always best to drive on (or off) at an angle to avoid 'grounding', the crew directing motorists into one of two or even three lanes of traffic to maximise capacity. Then, at the moment of departure, a black ball would be hoisted above the driver's cabin in the direction of travel. I'm sure I

*No doubt a cup of Van Houten's Cocoa would be particularly welcome in conditions such as those of 25 April, 1908! The unidentified tramcar stranded in the snow outside Plummer Roddis' store is of the knifeboard type common in Southampton until Percy Baker's domed roof design appeared in 1923. (Lens of Sutton)*

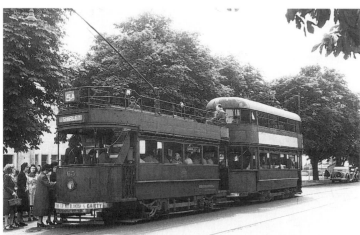

*Orchids for Miss Blandish was being advertised at The Gaiety in Southampton when these two trams were spotted in Commercial Road on 18 June, 1948. Open-top no. 65 was not attracting much custom on its knifeboard seating upstairs, but the domed car in front seems quite full. Route 5A ran from the docks to Shirley. Both tramcars retained their wartime grey paintwork, and were most likely withdrawn in that state the following year. (A.B. Cross)*

*The original Guy Arab was not very common in the South, but its acquisition from 1934 onwards by Southampton Corporation spelled the end of petrol-driven double-deckers. The Park Royal bodywork on no. 19 (OW 7239), new in 1935, lasted throughout this vehicle's 15-year life. The wide radiator was very different from utility and post-war Guys. (D. Kaye)*

*Diesel-operated floating bridge no. 12 is seen crossing the Itchen from west to east from no. 14, heading in the opposite direction. On the right the new road bridge nears completion, which spelled the end in 1977 for these quaint forms of municipal transport.*

speak for many when I say that there was a fascination in the gurgling and clanking sounds that emanated from the Bridge as it gathered way, the steel cables (or 'wires') groaning as they were kept in place by the pulleys at either end. It had been even more interesting still in the Forties and Fifties, before I had a car, for that meant a bus journey on both shores of the river. On the eastern shore I used to arrive from Fareham on a Hants & Dorset lowbridge double-decker on service 80, which terminated at Woolston depot on the south side of Portsmouth Road. Across the road, right in front of the Floating Bridge, was the Southampton

Corporation bus station — it was possible to catch either a 1 or a 3 bus right the way round to Southampton via Northam, but I never did. As a pedestrian I could travel over to the western side for nothing on the Floating Bridge, and then choose which of the Corporation buses I fancied to take me into the centre. The choice lay between prewar Leyland 'Titan' TD4 and TD5 models and the postwar Guy 'Arab' examples: though both types were fitted with similar Park Royal bodywork, the older Leylands had a tinted glass on the driver's side between the cab and the passenger saloon, to avoid glare or reflection from the interior lights

The Corporation fleet included a number of Leyland Cub buses, all but one of which had oil engines for greater fuel economy. No. 53 (OW 7315) was waiting at Houndwell while working route 8 to Woolston via Chessel Avenue. This early post-war scene, showing the Haymarket public house, gives a good impression of the rather derelict appearance of much of Southampton at the end of hostilities. In the background is a Park Royal-bodied Leyland Titan bound for Woolston via Bitterne. (D. Kaye)

There was an air of desolation at the tramway terminus near the floating bridge — just some war-damaged buildings, grimy domed-roof trams and few private cars. In the background Central Bridge rose to clear the railway tracks near Southampton Terminus station. (A.B. Cross)

On the Woolston side of the Itchen two Guy Arab double-deckers are parked up, most likely to await the rush-hour. No. 87 (DTR 910) was one of the 1946 deliveries, while 241 (HTR 58) joined the Corporation fleet in 1952. Though both featured the Gardner 6LW diesel engine (8.4 litres), no. 87 was an 'Arab' II and 241 a Mark III model. Together they represent the standardised SCT motor bus fleet of Guys with Gardner engines and Park Royal bodywork. Points to note are minor styling differences, particularly around the windows, and the oval headlamps (which doubled as fog lamps!). (A.B. Cross)

*On the Southampton side of the Itchen, Corporation buses connected with the floating bridges. Double-deck services 1 and 3 were regularly worked by the pre-war Leyland Titan TD4 and TD5 models throughout the 1940s. No. 41 (BTR 70) was snapped by the attractive shelter in about 1948 while waiting the arrival of the next bridge from Woolston — the spare bridge can be seen on the left, out of the water. (D. Kaye)*

*In 1956/7 Southampton Corporation put into service three 31-seat Albion Nimbus vehicles. Always intended for one-man operation, they were ideal for the lightly loaded service 10 between Swaythling, Stoneham Cemetery and Allington Lane, as this route had to negotiate the low bridge beneath the railway. No. 257 (STR 700) shows it can manage a U-turn at the Burgess Road junction when setting off on another round trip from Swaythling in the 1960s.*

at night. It also made it more difficult to watch the speedometer when the bus was on the move! It always seemed that drivers started up the moment they saw the Floating Bridge arrive, for almost invariably there was a delay when one reached the bus stop while the next crew had their tea break...

Once or twice I walked to the original London & South Western Railway terminus station near the Docks. It had opened on 10 June, 1839, but gradually as time went by and more trains took the direct route through the tunnel via Southampton West (later Central station) it became something of an anachronism, closing from 5 September, 1966. This was inevitable once the former Great Western services to Newbury and Didcot or Swindon and Cheltenham Spa were withdrawn from 7 March, 1960 and 11 September, 1961, respectively. But before then, it was pretty quiet for long periods of the day. If one walked past Central Bridge there might be a locomotive being watered or turned on the turntable opposite the distinctive goods depot, or perhaps a little B4 0-4-0T could be waiting for a further

*Rebuilt Battle of Britain 4-6-2 no. 34090 Sir Eustace Missenden, Southern Railway, inches towards No. 3 Gate with a fully-fitted load of banana vans from Southampton Docks (Old Docks) to Nine Elms just five weeks before the end of steam on the Southern — 5 June, 1967. A flagman was required to control road traffic whenever a train needed to cross Canute Road in or out of the Docks, a practice that continued at least into the mid-1970s.*

*The New Docks (constructed during the Thirties) were linked to the original 19th century network of wharves by a single railway track. On 18 April, 1960, one of the American-built 0-6-0T locomotives acquired by the Southern after World War II (USA class no. 30067) trundled a transfer freight from the New Docks past the Royal Pier, while a Corporation Guy Arab gathers passengers for Swaythling on service 15A.*

*Town Quay shunter: designed as a 2-2-0T for light passenger work by Dugald Drummond in 1906, most of the C14s were sold to the Government in 1917. The three survivors from the class of ten were rebuilt as 0-4-0Ts for improved adhesion when shunting and lingered until the Fifties on humble duties around Southampton. No. 30589 acquired a B4-type chimney in its later days — it had been numbered 744 when new, then 0744 (on the duplicate list) and 3744 from 1931 until 1948. On 7 April, 1955, it was performing sporadic shunting, as usual, on the Town Quay and adjoining tracks.*

*Southampton Terminus in the days of steam: on a hot Saturday afternoon, former Great Western 0-6-0 no. 2221 raises the echoes when departing with the 4.56 pm for Newbury while, alongside, a 'U' 2-6-0 has another half-hour to waste at the head of the 5.28 pm stopping service to Portsmouth on 15 June, 1957.*

In far from ideal weather conditions, class E6 0-6-2T no. 32416 backs down the Eling Tramway across the High Street level crossing at Totton to shunt the tar sidings. This picture was taken in 1952, before these ex-LBSCR tank engines were displaced by new Ivatt-designed 2-6-2Ts — 32416 (plus 32412/3) shedded at Eastleigh.

The only narrow-gauge system working throughout the year in the Solent area is the Hythe Pier tramway. In this tranquil scene an almost empty tram approaches the landward end of the pier on a dull winter's day.

The Southern Railway had three twin-funnel ships for the Channel Islands services from Southampton, all completed by William Denny & Brothers Ltd. of Dumbarton around the 1930s. On 15 July, 1961, the Isle of Guernsey was berthed in the Old Docks at Southampton. Soon after, all railway-operated sailings to the Channel Islands were based at Weymouth using more modern vessels.

This delightful old snapshot brings to life the simple pleasure of a charabanc outing after World War I. This gleaming Maudslay was new in 1916 (registered number CR 4385) to Trade Cars of Southampton, and probably made many similar excursions to the New Forest. In April 1920, the vehicle became part of Bournemouth & District's fleet, shortly to be renamed Hants & Dorset. It is believed this charabanc was numbered 58 and lasted until 1925 — doubtless it kept the solid tyres to the end!

*This is the busy bus station at West Marlands in Southampton in 1954/5. There is not a single underfloor-engined vehicle in sight, but there are several pre-war Bristol K5G double-deckers. JT 9358 (formerly TD 654, then renumbered 1030 in 1950) has only recently been rebodied at Eastern Coachworks with a 60-seat high-bridge body of increased width (8 feet). The two Leyland Titan PD2 buses (the one nearest the camera is 1220; JEL 497) have the maker's own highbridge bodywork, but all the other vehicles appear to have ECW bodies of lowbridge pattern. Of the 18 buses in view, only one is a single-decker — a post-war Bristol 'L' on the 40A service from Nomansland. (P. Davies)*

spell of shunting in the sidings, but the most exciting moment for a train-spotter was likely to be the passage of an Ocean Liner Express or a well-laden freight across Canute Road to or from the Docks. Anything crossing Canute Road required the services of a flagman, generally preceded by the ringing of a handbell to warn road traffic — all reminiscent of 19th century practice! There were several tracks crossing the road, but the two at No. 3 Gate were the most important and the last to remain in use.

Until 1979 it was still theoretically possible to do a complete tour of both Old and New Docks before rejoining the main line at either Millbrook or Northam, although transfer freights between the two had ceased by that time; the roadside track past the Town Quay and Royal Pier was severed shortly after. Though the latter lost its passenger services long ago, at the time of World War I, the Town Quay remained in business for goods until 1967. Small locomotives were needed to cope with the sharp radius curves on to the Quay,

*On 23 July, 1955, the 9.40 am Brighton to Bournemouth West through train was entrusted to class H2 4-4-2 Atlantic no. 32426 St. Alban's Head, while a London-bound express ran into platform 1 at Southampton Central behind Bulleid Light Pacific no. 34109, Sir Trafford Leigh-Mallory. Both locomotives have safety valves lifting ready for a prompt departure on one of the busiest days of the year.*

but they could cause chaos when shunting wagons out into Platform Road.

A useful but seldom photographed bus service used to connect the main (Central) station with Royal Pier. Operated by Hants & Dorset from the late-1940s until about 1980, it presented an interesting spectacle over the years with Dennis 'Ace', Leyland 'Cub', Bristol 'L' types and even 'MW' saloons eventually. Many of the vehicles were superannuated coaches but in more recent times Marchwood

Motorways has taken over the route. At Royal Pier a link is made with Red Funnel steamers to the Isle of Wight, and also with the Hythe Pier Ferry. The former provides an important passenger and vehicular service between the mainland and Cowes, Isle of Wight, whereas the latter offers local travellers an unhurried cruise down Southampton Water with excellent views to port and starboard. All the company's ferries are named 'Hotspur', and it also owns the narrow-gauge electric system that operates along the 700-yard Hythe Pier.

*Coal traffic was not what one normally associated with the Fawley branch — certainly not 43 wagonloads of it! On 6 March, 1960, a special test train was assembled behind class H16 4-6-2T no. 30516, to ascertain whether useful economies could be made by transferring some of the Pacific tanks to eliminate double-heading on petroleum traffic. The test was successful, as 30516 drifts into the terminus under light steam at the end of the run.*

Painted blue and cream, the tram looks delightfully quaint trundling to and fro above the waves. The tramway dates from 1922, but the Pier itself was built in 1880 and is owned by the General Estates Company Ltd.

It is interesting to reflect that, well within living memory, the double-tide waters of the Solent used to lap within yards of the railway just to the west of the present Southampton (Central) station. It was not until the 1930s that the Southern decided to develop that important site; widening the tracks, extending and modernising the station itself, building a bridge for road traffic that spanned the platforms and reclaiming much of the foreshore for new industrial purposes. But, of course, the Southern's predecessor in these parts — the London & South Western Railway — had acquired the original Southampton Docks Company as far back as 1892 and needed to expand its facilities for the new generation of world-class liners that were in prospect. Deep water berths, a new dry dock and miles of railway sidings took shape to the south of the power station and all along the foreshore as far as

Millbrook — the New Docks were born. On the other side of Southampton Water there was already a military port at Cracknore Hard, Marchwood, but it was not until the middle of World War II that it was connected to the rest of the railway system; the branch line from Totton to Fawley had been finally opened to traffic on 20 July, 1925, but passenger services were withdrawn again from 14 February, 1966. Freight business has continued to survive, with oil trains from the Fawley refinery forming the back-bone. Another curious survivor is the Eling Tramway branch. Open for freight for more than a century, the half-mile byway curves sharply back from beyond the Down platform at Totton station, crosses High Street with its hand-operated level crossing gates and throws off sidings to serve a number of industrial plants. One of my earliest photographs, taken on a prewar Coronet folding camera giving just eight 3" x 2" negatives on standard 120-size film, shows an E6 0-6-2T locomotive negotiating the crossing on a pick-up goods duty of the 1950s period, whereas today hefty diesels of classes 47 or 56 appear on stone trains.

*One of the most famous trains to be seen at Southampton until the end of steam was the Bournemouth Belle. Though the 12.30 pm from Waterloo was booked non-stop to Central station, it was not the fastest service because of the sheer weight of the luxurious Pullman cars. Near the end of its career, rebuilt West Country 4-6-2 no. 34026 Yes Tor still made an impressive sight as it restarted the heavy train from platform 4 on 27 March, 1966.*

I mentioned Hants & Dorset briefly earlier in the chapter. That company had begun modestly in the midst of World War I in the Bournemouth area trading as the 'Silver Fleet'. By 1920 its official title of Bournemouth & District did not properly reflect its burgeoning business, so the name was changed to Hants & Dorset Motor Services Ltd. It was in that year

it reached Southampton... An agreement with Elliott Brothers' old-established business allowed Hants & Dorset to concentrate on stage carriage services and not compete with Elliott's 'Royal Blue' on coaching activities. They cooperated on a joint bus and coach station in Bournemouth in 1931 but, only four years later, Elliott Brothers sold out to a consortium that included both Western/Southern National and Hants & Dorset. The former group took the express licenses and a proportion of the coaches while Hants & Dorset got some valuable premises and the rest of the coaches for excursion work.

After a short period of duplication with Elliott's former trading name, Western and Southern National coaches ran their express services as 'Royal Blue' and Hants & Dorset repainted those coaches they intended to retain (some being first rebodied by Beadle) into their own special livery of two shades of green and cream. Also in 1935 Hants & Dorset acquired another Southampton-based concern, Tourist Coaches, after a similar deal and division of spoils with Western/Southern National;

more property was involved, enabling Hants & Dorset to put up a purpose-built bus garage and workshop at Grosvenor Square while a coach station used by Royal Blue was built around the corner in Bedford Place. A Bus Station was approved on a site at West Marlands, near the Civic Centre, which achieved its objective of getting most of the company's vehicles off the streets of Southampton. Just think how much of W.W. Graham's careful enterprise during the 1920s and 30s was unravelled in the 1980s: first the disappearance of the Hants & Dorset name after the break-up of the National Bus Company, then de-regulation and finally the new game of asset-stripping, which has had the side-effect of flooding the streets with buses...

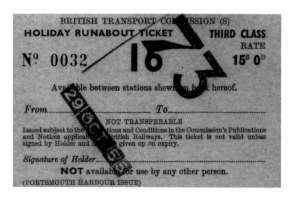

# 3 · INTERLUDE
## *On the Isle of Wight*

Not until the end of World War II in 1945 could my parents take me on a day trip to the Isle of Wight. Though I am unable to quote chapter and verse as to when it was, exactly, the opportunity to watch the coal-fired paddle steamer perform at close quarters was an experience never to be forgotten. The old Southern Railway vessel was nearing the end of its working life, having survived the dark days of the war crossing the Solent regularly between Portsmouth Harbour and Ryde Pier Head, but to a child it represented one of the wonders of the world! PS Merstone was my first experience of the breed and, though it has long since gone to a scrapyard fate, that name remains for ever etched in my memory.

Certainly there was very little to distinguish a journey to the Island in 1945 from how it must have been forty or fifty years before. The pace of change before the Age of Television was much slower, and on an island separated from the mainland by a strip of water that took half-an-hour to cross, innovation came not only even more sluggishly but it was generally secondhand as well! Rails first came to the Isle of Wight in 1862, when the Cowes & Newport Railway opened on 16 June. Two years later the Isle of Wight Railway inaugurated the line between Ryde (St. John's Road) and Shanklin, which was soon extended beneath St. Boniface Down to Ventnor. Other sections followed, piecemeal, until the last segment — from Godshill through Whitwell and St. Lawrence to Ventnor (West) — opened in 1900. With the

Grouping in 1923, the whole lot became part of the Southern Railway and fell under the remote control of Waterloo. Albums dealing specifically with the history of the Island railways show the amazing assortment of stock that the Southern inherited, much of it passed down from larger concerns on the mainland, but that is the way things have continued ever since. Many of the engines were given names of places on the Island, and when the Southern initiated some semblance of order and standardisation there, the practice was maintained — indeed, every locomotive numbered between 1 and 36 got a name! In the process of weeding out, the Southern Railway discovered some of Stroudley's famous A1/A1x 'Terrier' 0-6-0T locomotives such as were used on the Havant to Hayling branch on the mainland. Most were shipped back across the Solent, although two survived on the Island until 1949 in charge of the Ventnor West branch: one even gained the distinction of being the only Stroudley locomotive to be painted in Bulleid's Malachite Green, a striking colour scheme that it retained for a year or two after repatriation with the BR number 32677 (it had been W13 'Carisbrooke'). The other non-standard engines from the small Island railways were steadily exchanged for a substantial number of ex-LSWR 02 0-4-4Ts, which became responsible for all regular passenger services until the end of steam on 31 December, 1966; when the last 'Terriers' were replaced in 1949, there were no less than 23 of Adams' 02 design working from Ryde and Newport depots. Finally, for freight traffic and

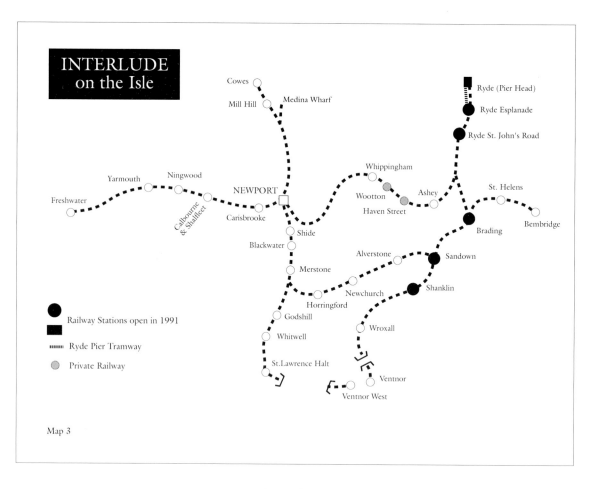

# INTERLUDE
## on the Isle

Cowes

Mill Hill

Medina Wharf

Ryde (Pier Head)

Ryde Esplanade

Ryde St. John's Road

Whippingham

Yarmouth

Ningwood

NEWPORT

Wootton

Ashey

St. Helens

Freshwater

Calbourne & Shalfleet

Carisbrooke

Haven Street

Brading

Bembridge

Shide

Blackwater

Merstone

Alverstone

Sandown

Newchurch

Shanklin

Horringford

Godshill

Wroxall

Whitwell

St.Lawrence Halt

Ventnor

Ventnor West

● Railway Stations open in 1991

■ Ryde Pier Tramway

◉ Private Railway

Map 3

*Electrified in 1886, Ryde Pier tramway boasted some quaint rolling stock for its half-mile line. The ornate tram further from the camera (known as the Grapes car) is preserved in Hull Museum. (Lens of Sutton)*

*Near the end of a long and honourable career, PS Ryde berths at Ryde Pier Head on 22 August, 1968. From here passengers from the mainland could catch a steam train to Ventnor or Cowes, take the tram to the Esplanade or just stroll along the Pier.*

occasional relief passenger duties on the summer-only 'Tourist' train, four of the six-coupled E1 tanks were brought over. Thus, from 1949 until 1966 the Isle of Wight managed quite successfully with just two types — all the engines having been built before the turn of the century, but equipped with larger coal bunkers necessary for the more intensive duties that characterised a popular holiday area.

Of the rolling stock, some four-wheeled carriages lingered until 1936 but the Southern's policy was to upgrade all lines with bogie vehicles as soon as practicable. Following electrification of the Portsmouth Direct and the coastal line to Brighton (now known as Coastway West), it was possible to cascade some older non-corridor bogies across the Solent before World War II; it was this type that

The legendary Bristol K5G, CDL 899, that Southern Vectis purchased new in 1939. In this Fifties picture taken at Ryde, by then numbered 702, the bus was working on route 4 from East Cowes. Being fitted with a highbridge Eastern Coachworks body, it was restricted mostly to services between Ryde, Newport and Cowes where there were no low railway bridges; it was converted to open-top in 1959. (D. Clark)

The only all-Leyland double-deckers to be seen on the Isle of Wight in post-war years were a pair of lowbridge Titan PD2s owned by Seaview Services. In the twilight of its working life, GDL 764 was to be found at Ryde Esplanade on 17 September, 1967, the dented roof indicating some of the problems on rural routes even for low-height double-deckers from overhanging trees. Retired in 1970, this fine machine stood out of use for many years before being preserved and restored again during the 1980s.

lasted to the very end of steam, antique but comfortable enough for fairly short journeys from Ryde to Sandown, Shanklin and Ventnor or northwards to Newport and Cowes. The goods wagons were equally venerable, and a mid-1960s freight train between Ryde St. John's and Medina Wharf offered an observer the vision of something preserved as if in aspic from the Edwardian period. This was the more remarkable since, on the mainland, fitted wagons and freightliners were about to become 'all the rage'. Fortunately, some representative examples of both locomotives and rolling stock from the 'steam' era have survived to be cherished there as part of the Isle of Wight's own microcosm of railway development: having been confined for some years to the mile or so of single line between Haven Street and Wootton, track is now being extended southwards through Ashey towards Smallbrook Junction where, with the active support of BR, a joint inter-change station is to be constructed in the 1990s. Ironically, only a few miles away on the banks of the Medina River can be seen the last example of a Southern Railway paddle-steamer. PS Ryde was built just before the outbreak of World War II, then called up for active service as a minesweeper (as HMS 'Ryde') before being allowed to resume more appropriate duties across the Solent until 1970. Like PS Merstone, it remained a coal-burner to the end of its days and is one of the select band of survivors of steam packet vessels that were so much a part of Britain's coastal scene in living memory. With a revival in the fortunes of the Island's railway, it would be wonderful if PS Ryde could sail across the Solent once more, resplendent in its classic Southern Railway livery?

One aspect of the transport system on the Isle of Wight that no longer exists, but which will not be forgotten by anyone who travelled to Ryde before 1967, is the Pier Tramway. This ran parallel to the railway for half-a-mile from the steamer berths at one end of the Pier to the Esplanade at the other. Always double track, the tramway was opened in 1864 and extended to St. John's Road in 1871, to connect with the trains. But, just as they had done on the mainland, both the London & South Western and London, Brighton & South Coast Railway jointly sought powers to enable a proper railway linking the Pier Head with the other lines at St. John's Road to be built. This involved tunnelling with a gradient as steep as 1 in 50, and the new route was opened on 12 July, 1880, though it meant abandonment of the tramway except on the Pier itself. The trams were initially horse-drawn, but the system was electrified in 1886 after a brief flirtation with steam haulage. Curiously, two petrol-driven railcars built by Drewry replaced the electric trams in 1927; they, in turn, were converted to diesel power after the war but were withdrawn when former London tube stock took over the Ryde - Shanklin remnant in 1967. The only survivor of the tramway today is the 'Grapes' car preserved at Hull.

Road transport, even in the towns, remained primitive for rather longer on the Island than was the case elsewhere. This was due in part to the lack of any street tramways (other than the one at Ryde, mentioned above), so a bold attempt by the Isle of Wight Express Motor Syndicate Ltd. to pioneer motor bus services in 1905 was unfortunate when it failed after just a couple of years. It was not until the inter-war period that buses flourished, leading to the formation in 1929 of the Southern Vectis Omnibus Company Ltd., as the major operator on the Island. I shall not attempt to cover that company's history as it has been detailed recently in Richard Newman's excellent volume, *Southern Vectis - The first 60 years* ( published by Ensign Publications but available direct from SVOC ). But the fleet has

On a scorching hot, August Bank Holiday weekend in 1969, one of the earliest Bristol Lodekka buses to reach Southern Vectis was waiting for custom at Ryde Esplanade with every window wide open. Numbered 504, this particular LD6G had the registration KDL 1 — a most eye-catching plate that was transferred to a private car when the bus went for scrap!

Three full-fronted open-toppers were obtained from Hants & Dorset in 1964. Formerly no. 1126, GLJ 969 was numbered 911 by Southern Vectis but there was no change of livery. Pounding up the 1 in 5 from Shanklin Esplanade in 1st gear, the Bristol K5G gave the conductor time to collect the fares! This was the scene on 18 May, 1970.

A more conventional open-top Bristol crossed the Solent to join Southern Vectis in 1964. New to Hants & Dorset in 1940, FLJ 538 was rebodied by ECW with a wider, highbridge convertible design in 1954. After an incident at Fareham, the bus became a permanent open-top before leaving the mainland (it was 1086 in the Hants & Dorset fleet). As no. 908 on the Island, it mostly worked between Yarmouth and Alum Bay on the seasonal service 42. On 1 September, 1969, it was negotiating the narrow bridge across the River Yar returning from Freshwater.

always had a close association with the railway, a feature that has become even more important since line closures in the Fifties and Sixties. A tangible connection with the olden days exists in the shape of a Bristol K5G double-deck bus, CDL 899: new in 1939 as a conventional highbridge vehicle, twenty years later its Eastern Coachworks body was converted to open-top and it continues to operate every season as a tourist attraction. In 1989 it was given a thorough overhaul and repaint to mark its Golden Jubilee, though it is now numbered 502 instead of 702 and no longer has the distinctive red destination blinds at one time unique to Island open-toppers.

Like most Southern Vectis buses purchased new until the latter part of the 1950s, CDL 899 has only a 12v electrical system. This means, in effect, that a mere car battery is asked to turn over 7 litres of high compression diesel engine! While this does not present much difficulty in the warmer summer months, especially if the driver remembers to push up the 'cold start' button under the bonnet, even a pair of hefty 6-volt batteries struggle to spin round the shaft of a Gardner diesel when temperatures are hovering at or below freezing. On the other hand, as half the Vectis fleet was laid up each winter, a reduction of 50% in the outlay on new batteries could prove a useful economy, and may well have contributed to the company's survival in a competitive world. Just once have I had the privilege of driving CDL, and found it a very stimulating experience: the testing technique of a 'crash' gearbox was mitigated somewhat by an effective clutch-stop apparatus, and with care I was able to produce quiet gear changes both upwards and downwards. One is helped on such a bus by an overall slow speed — it will only manage 29 mph in top gear on the level — but it was designed for the short journeys and hilly environment of the Isle of Wight where speed

has never been a necessary ingredient. Anyone who has been fortunate enough to sample a trip from Shanklin Esplanade up the 1 in 5 gradient to the town with a full complement of passengers on board will know how well this old Bristol 'K' can cope with such a severe test, even though it has a 5-cylinder engine and no chance of changing out of 1st gear on that tortuous, winding ascent! It is a measure of the high regard in which Gardner diesel engines were (and still are) held that Southern Vectis largely standardised on them in various configurations during the Forties, Fifties and Sixties, no matter whether the chassis was Dennis, Guy, AEC, Bristol or even Leyland.

Over the years, Southern Vectis has absorbed most of the other bus and coach operators on the Island. But Seaview Services remained independent, its striking colour scheme of two shades of green plus red standing out against the sober livery worn by its vastly bigger rival. After peace was declared in 1945 I used to look forward to at least one visit to the Island every summer. My first visit to Seaview itself was by Southern Vectis, and I still have the Bell Punch Automaticket that was completed by hand for service 7 from Ryde on the single-deck pre-war Bristol bus. But in later years I travelled on one or other of the fine pair of lowbridge all-Leyland 'Titan' PD2 double-deckers (GDL 764 and 765) that used the toll road via Puckpool Park to Seaview. One of them was replaced by a 3-axle Bedford VAL single-decker in 1964, but GDL 764 soldiered on to a ripe old age before being put out to grass; fortunately it not only survived, but has been restored and now appears at local rallies to the delight of more mature enthusiasts.

Before returning from this brief visit to the Island, one other transport phenomenon there should be mentioned. Although Red

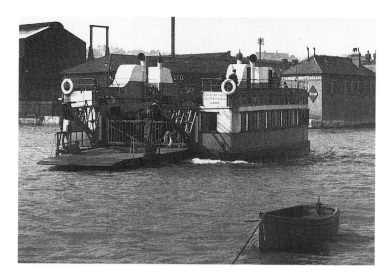

*A 1930s view of the floating bridge across the Medina River, between West and East Cowes. A modern version is still in operation today. (The News, Portsmouth)*

*Below : The deep shadows of a bright winter's day spell the end of steam for British Railways' Isle of Wight enclave. On the last day, 31 December, 1966, class 02 0-4-4T no. 17 (formerly Seaview) hisses exuberantly in a brave show at the head of a Ryde to Shanklin service as it passes a train for the opposite direction at Sandown station. Heads crane, cameras click, but the third rail is in place and this was supposed to be steam's sunset!*

*After their immaculate appearance in the early post-war years, the Island steam engines became increasingly decrepit during the 1960s. A class O2 0-4-4T, no. 26 Whitwell, shrouded in generous quantities of steam when restarting a Ryde — Cowes train from Ashey station on 3 October, 1965. The main building had become unsafe, so a temporary platform was erected on the opposite side of the track. Now there are plans to reinstate services between Wootton, Haven Street, Ashey and Smallbrook Junction using veteran Victorian steam locomotives and period Island rolling stock.*

Funnel steamers operate from Southampton to both West and East Cowes, a Floating Bridge plies across the Medina River, linking the two. This was originally established in the 1850s but was leased by the operator of the Southampton - Cowes steamships in 1882.

The Floating Bridge is now controlled by the Isle of Wight County Council.

But even as the old coal-fired paddle steamers, which had their origins in the technology of the 19th century, were being phased

*In their heyday the Island '02' tanks had coped with prodigious loads of holiday-makers from the mainland at the height of the season. In this July 1963 picture, no. 31 Chale sets off from Ryde Pier Head with at least five non-corridor bogies bound for Sandown, Shanklin and Ventnor; the Drummond boiler fitted to this engine was one of a pair circulated among the Adams '02' class on heavy overhaul at the works. Note the signal cabin controlling all movements at the Pier Head's four platforms, and the tramway tracks in the foreground. .*

out, so the 1960s saw the arrival of both hover-craft and hydrofoil for the comparatively short crossing of the Solent. Hydrofoil have become the speciality of the Red Funnel group and provide a quick means of transit between Southampton and Cowes, for those who want speed. Another company — Hovertravel Ltd — has opted for the hovercraft exclusively on its route between Ryde and the mainland. At one time in the Sixties crossings (or 'flights') were made alternatively from Ryde to Southsea (Clarence Pier) or Stokes Bay, but the latter was abandoned after just a few seasons. I well remember one visit to the Island when the Solent was distinctly choppy; with weather conditions deteriorating as the day wore on, it seemed sensible to return home earlier than intended and the quickest way from Ryde was by hovercraft. Although I had set out from Portsmouth, as the first available hovercraft flight back was to Stokes Bay I decided not to linger — conscious of the advice of Lady Macbeth "Not to stand upon the order of (one's) going, but go at once!" Other intending passengers took a similar view and the small SRN6 was soon well-laden. With power on, it swung round on the launch pad on the beach at Ryde scattering shingle in its haste, then took the shortest route across the Solent. The wind came in gusts, with waves sometimes breaking over the little craft as it caught a heavy swell.

The stench of kerosene pervaded the saloon (or cabin) and did nothing to help one's stomach come to terms with a very lively crossing indeed! But while it was not an experience to be repeated — subsequent flights were suspended due to the adverse weather conditions — the pilot could not be faulted for his skill in bringing the hovercraft safely on to the beach at Stokes Bay. Luckily, I have a colour transparency taken in much better conditions to record that short-lived experiment.

With new technology threatening to eat into British Railways' traditional monopoly between Portsmouth and the Isle of Wight — they ran the car ferry service from Broad Street, Old Portsmouth, to Fishbourne in addition to the passenger ferry, long before Sealink or Wightlink were dreamt of — Southern Region tried out a small, fast craft of their own across the Solent. Nicknamed by some the 'plastic duck', it operated (as far as I am aware) only between Portsmouth and Ryde Pier Head, using the traditional steamer berths, as a supplementary facility for anyone wanting a quicker journey. It was not a hovercraft nor a hydrofoil but, like both, combined a speedier crossing with limited accommodation and basic comfort; it had a fairly short working life during the latter part of the 1960s, and I have no photograph of it in my collection. That's life!

# 4 · ALL AROUND POOLE BAY
## *From Portland to Lymington*

Since closure of the Freshwater, Yarmouth and Newport branch line on the Isle of Wight from 21 September, 1953, there has been no rail link for passengers wanting to use the Yarmouth to Lymington ferry across the Solent. On the mainland though, the single-track branch to Brockenhurst continues to thrive, in spite of a number of changes. Its origins are of respectable antiquity; opened between Lymington Junction, on the 1847 'Castleman's Corkscrew' route west from Southampton to Ringwood and Dorchester, to a temporary terminal at Lymington on 12 July 1858, it soon warranted the fine building that still constitutes the Town station (built in 1860). Ever conscious of the lure that the Isle of Wight held for holidaymakers, especially since Queen Victoria and her family spent so much time at Osborne House, the LSWR extended the branch across the river a further half-mile to Lymington Pier to enable easier connections to be made with the steam packet boat to Yarmouth, on 1 May, 1884. In July of the same year the Railway took over operation of the ferry service, thus providing a unified rail/ferry/rail link similar to that available from London to Portsmouth and Ryde. When the railway between Newport, Yarmouth and Freshwater closed at the end of the 1953 season it was only to be expected that vehicular traffic needed to expand if the route was to remain viable, so larger ferries were introduced to encourage this development. In 1980 the Lymington - Yarmouth route celebrated 150 years of operation, but with the sale of

British Railways' shipping interests during the Eighties, it became part of the international Sea Containers Group. Recently, the Sealink element of that organisation has been resold so the 'railway connection' is now a thing of the past.

From 5 March, 1888, a new direct route between Southampton and Bournemouth was inaugurated when the line from Brockenhurst through Sway to Christchurch was opened to traffic. Previously, passengers for Bournemouth had to travel round via Wimborne, Broadstone Junction and Poole. Alternatively, it was possible to reverse at Ringwood and use the branch line via Hurn to Christchurch (opened on 13 November 1862). From 14 March 1870 it was extended through Boscombe to the new coastal resort amid the pine trees. As the rail journey to Bournemouth in the 1870s was slow and tedious, the Elliott family began their famous 'Royal Blue' coaching service by 1880, in order to provide a direct connection from Holmsley station — originally known as Christchurch Road — for the well-to-do clientele. But developments came quickly: a new terminus at Bournemouth West had opened on 15 June 1874 and only a month later the Somerset & Dorset Bath Extension route came into existence. By November 1886 through trains were possible from Bath (Green Park) to Bournemouth without reversal at Wimborne by using the new cut-off line through Corfe Mullen to Broadstone Junction. Particularly in summer, this improvement resulted

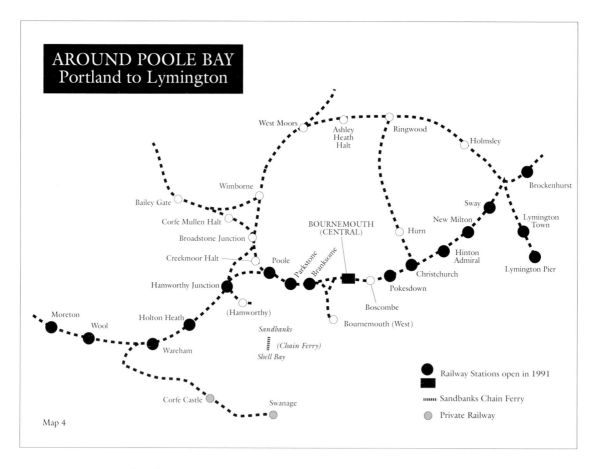

AROUND POOLE BAY
Portland to Lymington

West Moors
Ashley Heath Halt
Ringwood
Holmsley
Wimborne
Bailey Gate
Corfe Mullen Halt
Broadstone Junction
BOURNEMOUTH (CENTRAL)
Hurn
Sway
New Milton
Brockenhurst
Lymington Town
Creekmoor Halt
Poole
Parkstone
Branksome
Hinton Admiral
Lymington Pier
Hamworthy Junction
Christchurch
Pokesdown
(Hamworthy)
Boscombe
Moreton
Wool
Holton Heath
Bournemouth (West)
Sandbanks
(Chain Ferry)
Wareham
Shell Bay

● Railway Stations open in 1991
■ 
▦ Sandbanks Chain Ferry
◉ Private Railway

Corfe Castle
Swanage

Map 4

On a misty Sunday morning in December, 1963 the branch train gets ready for the day's activities at Lymington Town. While a watery sun makes patterns through the smoke and steam, class M7 0-4-4T no. 30480 shunts the push-pull carriages past the train shed before propelling them over the bridge to Lymington Pier station.

*With the sun low in the western sky, 'M7' 0-4-4T no. 30379 bustles over the bridge across the Lymington River in early April 1963, at the head of a branch train for Brockenhurst. Though it was a single line, it was signalled throughout.*

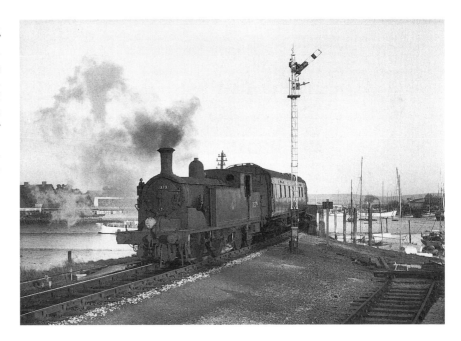

in the steady expansion of traffic from the Midlands, South Wales and the North filtering on to the jointly-owned Somerset & Dorset at Bath, where reversal was always necessary to the end of its days. The LSWR capitalised on the growing popularity of Bournemouth both by the new direct route from London and in forming a pact with the Midland Railway to manage the precarious Somerset & Dorset together; it proved to be a profitable investment.

As Bournemouth, with its historic neighbouring town of Christchurch, grew and expanded westwards to embrace the more industrial ports of Hamworthy and Poole a network of local transport began to emerge. It was from the last-mentioned town that the impetus came, with the Poole & District Electric Traction Company commencing tramway operation from the railway station to County Gates via Upper Parkstone. When attempts were made to extend across the county boundary into Bournemouth itself (and beyond) difficulties arose.

Bournemouth Corporation changed its mind about the need for trams and embarked on its own system within the borough. After the inevitable legal wrangles, a compromise was reached that resulted in the Bournemouth Corporation Tramways Act of 1903 whereby the Poole line was leased to Bournemouth for 30 years and the whole system became unified from 3 July, 1905. When the extension to Christchurch was constructed later that year the line from Poole right through to its new terminus adjacent to the ancient Priory became the longest in Southern England (outside London), in excess of 11 miles. The gauge of the Bournemouth tramways was 3 ft. 6 inches, instead of the more usual 'standard' width of 4 ft. 7·75 inches (compatible with railway tracks of 4 ft. 8·5 inches) found at Portsmouth, Southampton and Gosport (after electrification).

With continuing growth in the local population, public transport expanded to keep

*An interesting microcosm of rural Dorset in about 1900: two Royal Blue carriages belonging to Elliott Brothers have called at a country hostelry to enable the passengers to take some refreshment, while two bicycling enthusiasts proudly show off their machines for the photographer. The inn offered 'celebrated Ales & Stout' from Blandford Brewery, but despite careful research it has not been possible to locate the site.*

*The Corporation tramway terminus in Church Street, Christchurch, in the Edwardian era. Car no. 2 has just arrived from Poole and passengers are about to get off; others, suitably wrapped up for their journey, wait in the roadway outside Froud Bros. (Boot Maker). A horse-drawn conveyance stands outside the Dolphin Inn on the opposite side of the street. (Lens of Sutton)*

*Still showing signs of its wartime livery, Corporation trolleybus no. 120 (ALJ 994) was pictured at The Square in the summer of 1950. It was one of the large contingent of Park Royal-bodied Sunbeam MS2 vehicles obtained in 1935, whereas behind stood the experimental Sunbeam (no. 68: LJ 7701) from the original quartet of trolleys tested in 1933; it had a Weymann body. Both were withdrawn in 1952, but many pre-war trolleys lingered on into the 1960s. (A.B. Cross)*

being designed as the 1930s approached. They also took powers to experiment with trolleybuses after one of the tram routes was closed and replaced by Hants & Dorset vehicles. The trolley experiment began on 13 May, 1933, and was an instant success between Bournemouth Square and Westbourne. As Poole Borough Council would not agree to trolleybuses on its side of the boundary, trams between Poole and Westbourne were replaced from 8 June 1935, by green and cream Hants & Dorset double-deck buses. From Westbourne eastwards through Bournemouth to Christchurch the trams gave way to a vast fleet of yellow Sunbeam trolleybuses after 8 April, 1936. One result of this changeover was the need to construct a turntable at Christchurch for the new vehicles to turn round in a very limited area — something that had not been necessary with tramcars. The turntable remained a feature of the Bournemouth system throughout the years of trolleybus operation, and was not removed until the old terminus near the Priory was abandoned in the Seventies. Several excellent publications on the former Corporation tramway and trolleybus system have been published by its successor, Bournemouth Transport, which today trades as Yellow Buses from its depot at Mallard Road. In recent times an associated concern, Yellow Coaches, has been established for private hire and express operations far

pace with it. Though there were some extensions to the tramways, it was the more flexible motor buses that spread to all the new estates beyond the coastal strip. Bournemouth Corporation had experimented with a solitary Berna bus from 1906, in the summer season only, but no serious attempt to operate an alternative to the trams was made until the 1920s. By this time other bus and coach companies, among them Hants & Dorset and Wilts & Dorset, were growing rapidly. The former, especially, was opening up new routes all along the coast as well as inland. To counter this competition, Bournemouth Corporation began to purchase larger numbers of the more reliable buses

Memorable excursion coach: Southdown Leyland Tiger TS8 no. 1212 (EUF 512) was supplied with the 8.6 litre diesel engine from new in 1938. This vehicle retained its sleek Harrington body, complete with sliding roof and semaphore trafficators, throughout its 18-year life with the company. What a civilised way to enjoy a day out in Bournemouth, whether in 1938 or 1950 — or even 1993!

One of the 'anonymous' Bournemouth Corporation Leyland Tiger PS2s with full-fronted Burlingham coachwork, used on the summer-only service 15 (the circular tour) from the Pier, photographed when almost new. After its first repaint in 1952, JLJ 401 was given fleet numbers at front and rear (44). The roof must be open on this occasion, as the sun is illuminating the seats inside quite clearly. (A.B. Cross)

The utility-bodied Bristol 'K' buses of Hants & Dorset were always as-sociated with Bournemouth. Fitted with 55-seat lowbridge body by Strachans, FRU 303 was the first of this batch to arrive in October 1944. It was originally numbered TD 772 in the fleet, but became 1106 in 1950 — when it was spotted head-ing for the Bus Station in Exeter Road on service 5 from Poole. An AEC 7.7 litre engine was fitted at this stage. (A.B. Cross)

Around the edge of the open part of the bus station at Bournemouth, spare vehicles were parked, such as this Bristol L6G of Black & White (no. 94: CDG 371) and Leyland Tiger TS7 of Hants & Dorset (CEL 229). The latter had the stylish Beadle semi-streamlined coachwork made famous by the Bournemouth-based company. Who would have guessed that CEL 229, recently renumbered 627 instead of F564, had only a few weeks left in service in the summer of 1950? The Eastern Coachworks-bodied Bristol, on the other hand, outlasted its contemporary by a further six years, but it did have the benefit of a diesel engine. (A.B. Cross)

Just returned after 15 months on loan to London Transport, no. 1180 (HLJ 37) roars past a Royal Blue relief in Exeter Road, Bournemouth in the summer of 1950. The Bristol K6A was part of a large order for new double-deckers that was diverted direct from the bodybuilder (ECW), so its original fleet number, TD888, was never seen in its home area as renumbering occurred on 1 January, 1950. The AEC Regal (1060: ETA 994) had been rebodied by Beadle the previous year — it's interesting to note that both vehicles had the same type of engine, the AEC 7.7 litre 6-cylinder diesel. (A.B. Cross)

Numerically the last of the full-fronted Leyland Titan TD5 double-deckers purchased in 1939, no. 32 (FEL 215) was still fitted with a petrol engine and sunroof when this view was taken outside Southcote Road depot on 15 June, 1948. Later this bus was converted to diesel and, later still, rebuilt with single staircase as an open-topper for the Coastal Service from Alum Chine to Hengistbury Head. It is believed to be still in existence in East Anglia. (A.B. Cross)

*One of the remarkable utility Guy Arab buses that served Bournemouth Corporation for 20 years. No. 35 (FRU 182) was delivered in 1943, being one of the initial batch of 500 Guys built for the war effort — subsequently known at Mark Is. It retained its Park Royal body till withdrawal in 1963 and always had large headlamps; a Gardner 6LW engined provided ample power. It was photographed at The Triangle on 15 August, 1953. (A.B. Cross)*

allowed to come home from primary school unaccompanied. So much so that, if I wasn't home at the expected time, my mother took to ringing up the Garage to remind me that tea was ready! Under the indulgent eye of the young lady in charge, I even learned how to operate the telephone switchboard. It was not uncommon for me to run home along Military Road clutching a timetable, ticket roll or other treasure pushed into my grubby hand by the kindly Beryl, along with the latest excursion handbill. This form of advertising bore fruit, for the trip to Bournemouth — with guaranteed 5-hour stay — made a great day out in the late-1940s. For anyone with an interest in buses, the place was an assured Mecca with Royal Blue express coaches, Corporation trolleys, Hants & Dorset buses and coaches and occasional examples from Bere Regis & District, Southern National and Wilts & Dorset on view.

beyond the confines of the erstwhile Borough of Bournemouth.

In the immediate post-war years it was a regular treat during school holidays or, when I had become a boarder at Churcher's College, at half-term, to be taken for a day out to Bournemouth. By 1946 Southdown Motor Services Ltd., had managed to reinstate a modest programme of half and whole day excursions for the summer season. Destinations varied week by week, simple typewritten leaflets being available from the enquiry office at Hilsea Garage. I had become a regular visitor to this fascinating place as soon as I was

Both of these last-mentioned companies had one stage carriage route each out of Bournemouth; Southern National to Weymouth, Wilts & Dorset to Salisbury, in either case joint with Hants & Dorset, and thus permitted to use the Bus Station off Exeter Road near the Square. The Southdown excursion coach itself could be a fine machine, perhaps one of the pre-war Harrington-bodied classics or a practically new post-war example with bodywork by Eastern Coachworks, Park Royal, Duple or Beadle. Though I was lucky

*The 2.35 pm (Sundays) stopping service from Bournemouth West to Southampton Central via Bournemouth Central, chirrups round the Branksome Triangle towards Gasworks Junction behind class 4MT 2-6-0 no. 76008 on 8 February, 1959. The Branksome sub-shed was behind the photographer but, on winter Sundays, no locomotives were active; two or three Somerset & Dorset engines were inside in light steam in readiness for Monday morning duties.*

enough to sample just about all of them over a period of five or six years, I especially remember one excursion with the unique Leyland 'Tiger' TS8 tourer, 1212 (EUF 512). It was the Whitsun weekend of 1950, when large numbers of the most modern coaches were required for express or relief duties, so for a leisurely excursion Hilsea Garage turned out this handsome 12-year old Harrington-bodied coach. Fitted with the 8.6 diesel engine since new, it nevertheless purred along effortlessly for mile after mile. We joined it at Fareham and had seats on the offside, near the front. The route was via Bursledon and then over Northam Bridge into Southampton — there was no M27 Motorway then! On through Millbrook, Redbridge and Totton the road was soon heading into the New Forest at Ashurst, then over the railway and straight on to Lyndhurst. There was always a short stop opposite the fire station with 10 minutes to stretch one's legs or get an ice cream in one of the shops. Sometimes two or three cows might

be wandering aimlessly through the main street, for they were less of a hazard when there were fewer vehicles on the roads. With everyone back aboard, 1212 got into its stride again; passing first over the 'Old Road' at Holmsley station and afterwards over the 'New Line' on the skew near Hinton Admiral, the coach ran into Christchurch, slowing for the Avon bridges before continuing to Iford Bridge across the Stour. Finally, it ran past Pokesdown trolleybus depot to the Lansdowne and along Bath Road, setting everyone down opposite the small Hants & Dorset depot close to the Pier.

We were about to cross the road to have a quick look at the former Elliott Brothers' 'Royal Blue' coach station, acquired by Hants & Dorset in 1935, when a stylish new vehicle in primrose yellow paintwork swept past and round the corner outside the Baths. It bore no fleet number like other Corporation buses, but the full-front cab with exposed radiator, rakish

*Rebuilt West Country class 4-6-2 no. 34018 Axminster drifts down through Parkstone station with the 10.30 am Waterloo — Weymouth train on 17 October, 1966. By this time the sidings to the goods yard (right) had been lifted. Although Waterloo to Bournemouth services were electrified from July 1967, trains to Weymouth had to wait another 20 years or so for the Wessex Electrics to arrive.*

lines and 'boat-tail' at the rear had the distinctive Burlingham shape. Looking back now, I can't think why I did not pester my long-suffering parent to have a ride on it; perhaps the family finances were unprepared for a call of that nature, or more likely there was so much else to see after a stroll through the gardens to the Square there might not have been time...

Certainly, since all Hants & Dorset vehicles had been renumbered on 1 January 1950, there was plenty to find of interest at the Bus Station adjoining Exeter Road. They had lost their quaint 'class' letters and numerals in favour of a new integrated system, with blocks of numbers from 500 upwards being allocated to particular types of bus, the numbers themselves appearing on neat little metal plates at front and rear. In the cases of older vehicles that had not been repainted, it was possible to see the transfer of the former fleet number daubed over on the bonnet side or below the rear window — in the absence of any handy pocket guide to Hants & Dorset by a certain well-known transport publisher, these observations were invaluable! Also, there were some vehicles operating in the Bournemouth area that were seldom, if ever, seen elsewhere. Utility Bristol 'K' and smart AEC 'Regent' double-deckers were particularly interesting, while some pre-war Leylands appeared on more humble duties. Last survivors also gravitated to Bournemouth, such as Dennis 'Ace' or Leyland 'Lion' models, soon to be replaced by little Bedford 'OB' buses or the ubiquitous Bristol 'L'. Some pre-war Leyland coaches, similar to our 1212 but with a very special design of Beadle bodywork, still undertook afternoon tours to Lulworth Cove — one or two even retained the smooth, near-silent but thirsty petrol engine in spite of fuel rationing — while a never-ending procession of Royal Blue coaches dived into the depths beneath the Bus Station on long distance express services to London, Portsmouth and all over the West. The majority were postwar Bristol 'L' machines with 5-speed gearboxes and coachwork by Beadle or Duple, but during the peak season they were augmented by some prewar AEC 'Regal' models and any number of 'hired in' coaches from an assortment of operators throughout the West Country. It was this policy that allowed Royal Blue its remarkable flexibility.

But Bournemouth Corporation did not run trolleybuses to the exclusion of almost anything else. At the Square there was a steady stream of them, naturally, still with brown roofs as a reminder of the war, but there were some motor buses at work as well. The first of the new Leyland 'Titan' PD2 double-deckers (KEL 110 etc.) had arrived and soon ousted the still petrol-engined pre-war 'Titan' TD5s from the prime route 1 to Christchurch and Purewell: both designs had full-fronted Weymann bodywork with twin staircases, a fetish that distinguished Bournemouth Corporation vehicles for many years. The TD5s had another very special feature that all but six retained to the end of their days — a sunroof! Built in 1939 to a lavish specification, they exchanged their extravagant petrol engines for diesels in the early 1950s, continuing in service until well into the 1960s; half a dozen were rebuilt to open-top for the summer coastal operation between Alum Chine and Hengistbury Head via the Piers and Overcliff Drive, losing the front staircase in order to increase seating capacity. There were a few more double-deck motor buses, including a handful of utility Guy 'Arab' models obtained in the war, but once the powerful PD2s came on the scene the others lapsed into obscurity. It was 1962 before I obtained a photograph of one of the Guys, still incredibly utilitarian but useful in the rush-hour; they had been the Corporation's first diesel buses.

Lastly, I must mention the little Bedfords. The Corporation had invested in two series of 'WTB' models with Burlingham 'Sun Saloon' bodywork, featuring curved glass panels and sliding roofs in 1938/9. Numbered between 1 and 16, they were used on a variety of tasks including the Coastal Service before open-top vehicles became available. During the war six more Bedfords arrived, but they were fitted with angular utility bodywork on the 'OWB' chassis. Despite this, four were subsequently rebuilt as open-toppers for seasonal use along the Undercliff Drive until displaced by a pair of 'Banana Boat' rebuilds of Guy 'Arab' double-deckers.

Soon after moving to Fareham in 1948 I became friendly with a boy of about my own age who was then living at Lee-on-the-Solent, where his father was a bank manager. By about 1953 they moved to Upper Parkstone, between Bournemouth and Poole, living in a flat over the bank. Occasionally I was invited to go and stay with the family for a weekend, either cycling the whole way (and back) through the New Forest or using the South Coast Express service. This was mostly a joint operation by Southdown and Royal Blue, but in summer coaches from East Kent and Maidstone & District could also be seen over sections of the route, which extended from Margate to Bournemouth. The advantage of a scheduled express service over a day excursion was its frequency: one could be picked up within walking distance of home (on the A27 at the foot of Titchfield Hill) and several ran daily, in each direction. During my visits to Parkstone he and I took every opportunity to try out public transport: for example, between Bournemouth Bus Station (and Royal Blue Coach Station) and Upper Parkstone the easiest way was by Hants & Dorset bus, as both services 3 and 4 stopped practically outside the bank. The regular type of bus for two decades was one of the rugged Bristol 'KSW' vehicles with highbridge double-deck body by Eastern Coachworks — Hants & Dorset had very good value out of them — although sometimes the duties might be shared with representatives of the dropped-chassis 'Lodekka' in its various forms. One of the pre-production prototypes of this design, the bus featured on all Bristol publicity material of the period, was no. 1337 (LRU 67); built in 1953, it spent most of its long working life based at Bournemouth and Poole. But one of the great attractions of the Bournemouth area, certainly until 1962, was the Somerset & Dorset railway line from Bournemouth West. It was not necessary to go back into Bournemouth to catch and Somerset & Dorset

train, unless perhaps one intended travelling on a summer Saturday, as most local services called at Branksome (handy for the small Somerset & Dorset loco depot, a sub-shed initially of the large establishment at Central station, 71B) or at Parkstone. The latter station was a formidable place for trains bound for Bournemouth to stop, as it was perched in the midst of the 1 in 60 gradient that prevailed for most of the way up from Poole to Branksome. But Parkstone was also notable for the little mineral railway that ran from the goods yard down to South Western Pottery. It boasted a delightful Peckett 0-4-0ST steam locomotive named "George Jennings", after the founder of the business; it was built in 1902 and lasted for 60 years.

Poole Harbour — what memories that name can conjure up! Sailing and shipping of all kinds have used this natural land-locked port for centuries, while the first recorded use of the coat of arms for the Borough of Poole occurred in 1371. The first railway reached the Hamworthy side of the harbour in 1847, as part of the Southampton & Dorchester Railway, and it was another quarter of a century before the main part of Poole had its own tracks extended from Broadstone Junction. By 1896 the original station on the Hamworthy side was closed to passengers, although the branch line from Hamworthy Junction still remains open for freight even today. But while there are railway tracks in place on the quay at Hamworthy, those that used to run through the streets of Poole to the Custom House became disused before the end of steam. On both sides of the harbour they were the preserve of tiny 0-4-0 tank locomotives, because of the sharp curves on the quays. But today a standard English Electric 350 hp diesel shunter handles the traffic up to the Junction.

Ten years after the "Castleman's Cork

screw" line opened for business came the extension to Weymouth from 20 January, 1857. Because the tracks of the Great Western Railway and its allies were constructed to the Broad Gauge (7 ft. and a quarter inch), it was necessary to employ mixed gauge between Dorchester and Weymouth. As Broad Gauge was doomed in Britain, the Great Western gave up the unequal struggle and, over a period of years, converted all its tracks to the generally accepted standard width of 4 ft. 8·5 inches. The LSWR cooperated with local interests in getting a branch line built from Worgret Junction, just west of Wareham, to Corfe Castle and Swanage; it was opened on 20 May 1885 and taken over by the South Western the following year. These are all the railway lines that are strictly relevant to the title of this volume, but I will just include two others on the Dorset coast that are closely involved with those already mentioned. These are the branches from Weymouth (Melcombe Regis) to Portland and Easton, another joint venture between the LSWR and GWR that had a rather complicated history and was not finally completed until 1900, and the Weymouth Quay tramway. The latter originated with the Great Western, initially for freight traffic in 1865 but also for passengers 24 years later when the railway took over the ships of the Weymouth and Channel Islands Steam Packet Company from 1 July, 1889. None of the railway routes mentioned above closed down until after the Beeching Plan of the 1960s, but passenger traffic was withdrawn from the Portland and Easton branch from 3 March, 1952; it was shut completely after the last freight from the Sheepcroft siding at Easton on 9 April, 1965. After withdrawal of all summer through trains from the Somerset & Dorset line on 8 September, 1962, it was only a matter of time before the rest of the traffic followed suit; closure was set for 3 January, 1966, but as certain replacement bus routes had not been authorised by that date a token service remained in force until 5 March. A final, nostalgic special for enthusiasts ran with a brace of Bulleid 'Light Pacifics' the following day. Although the Somerset & Dorset must have been an expensive line to maintain, no

*Centre : A return excursion from Bournemouth West to Weston-super-Mare takes the Sussex & Dorset line at Broadstone Junction on Easter Monday, 18 April, 1960. Armstrong 4F 0-6-0 no. 44557 is opened up as it passes the signal box, while the fireman watches carefully to ensure the single-line tablet for Corfe Mullen is collected as the eight-coach train accelerates away. This locomotive was built for the Somerset & Dorset Joint Rly is 1922 and absorbed by the LMS in 1930.*

*From the eastern edge of the Chesil beach at Fortuneswell, passengers on the little train between Portland and Weymouth had a fine view of the Bay and distant Purbeck Hills. Regular passenger traffic to Portland and Easton ceased in 1952, but 0-6-0PT no. 3737 was returning to Weymouth (Melcombe Regis) with an enthusiasts' special on 14 August, 1960.*

attempt was made to introduce a local diesel service to cut costs and increase patronage, while withdrawal of the holiday trains and through freight was the kiss of death for a route that could have made a great contribution to easing congestion on the roads... 20 years on. But if closure of the Somerset & Dorset was a tragedy, withdrawal of the passenger trains from Corfe Castle and Swanage was just absurd; the diesel multiple unit service ceased from 3 January 1972.

Before leaving the Isle of Purbeck and Poole Harbour it is time to return to the water.

The famous shipping concern of Cosens & Co. of Weymouth had been founded in the mid-19th century, in due course offering excursions to a number of South Coast resorts, as well as cross-Channel trips to Cherbourg and the Channel Islands. The company operated several paddle steamers over the years, but one of the best known must have been PS Empress, built in 1879. Based for some time at Bournemouth, the vessel was requisitioned during both World Wars but on each occasion was returned to Cosens after hostilities were over. Empress appeared in the classic film of Dickens' "Great Expectations" (which starred,

An abiding memory of the 'Silent Service' provided so ably by Bournemouth Corporation trolleybuses until 20 April, 1969 is this winter picture of Sunbeam MF2B no. 298 (298 LJ). One of the last trolleybuses to be built in Britain, featuring fluorescent lighting and bright, easy-to-clean interior decor, 298 entered service in the summer of 1962. The wet road and time-exposure combine to evoke an ethereal quality of a nocturnal journey from the Square to Tuckton Bridge on route 22; the date was 16 January, 1969.

Somerset & Dorset speciality: the 7.40 am (Saturdays only) through train from Birmingham (New Street) begins the assault on Parkstone Bank behind class 7F 2-8-0 no. 53800 on 2 August, 1958. Designed for the Somerset & Dorset freight traffic in 1914, the eleven members of this class were found to be capable of handling up to ten-coach loads un-aided to help out on summer weekend passenger duties in later years. The 1 in 60 of Parkstone Bank was the last adverse gradient before terminating at Bournemouth West, and required considerable skill to avoid over-firing in the final stages of a long run from Bath (Green Park). Hamworthy and Poole Gasworks are on the horizon.

among others, the young John Mills) and finally retired from cruising in 1955. Another paddle steamer, whose appearance was all the more familiar having been built for the ferry service between Portsmouth and Ryde but under a different name, was the Embassy. Apart from the white funnel, Embassy looked very much at home among the other ex-Southern Railway vessels - Ryde, Sandown, Whippingham, Shanklin and Merstone — in the late-1940s and 1950s. For all our modernisation and affluence, the simple pleasure of a cruise around the Solent or along the coast on board a stately old paddle steamer any day during the season has been lost to us. But today's motorists can still savour one mainland Floating Bridge, if they don't mind the queues and a toll road.

This runs from Sandbanks, a long spit of land between Bournemouth and Poole, across the narrow entrance of the outer harbour to Shell Bay. It was opened in 1925 and still runs on chains because of the strong tidal currents. Originally employing a steam bridge, the link is now maintained by a diesel. As there is only one bridge, in the event of maintenance or repairs being needed all traffic is obliged to use the much longer way round via Wareham. An interesting feature of the Sandbanks Ferry is its use by an hourly bus service to and from Swanage via Studland. Although visiting coaches have been known to travel on the Floating Bridge, some care needs to be exercised when boarding or leaving the vessel because of the steep ramps; regular buses over the years have had modifications made to the front and back to avoid any risk of grounding. The route was reinstated by Hants & Dorset using petrol-engined Leyland 'Lion' LT5A saloons immediately after World War II, but those delightful vehicles gave way to diesel-engined Bristol 'L5G' single-deckers by 1951. While it was possible to employ a 30 feet long vehicle after suitable modification, versions of the 'L' type continued to be responsible for day to day operations on route 7 via the Sandbanks Ferry until 1970.

And so what began as a day excursion to Bournemouth has turned into a broad review of most forms of public transport in West Hampshire and East Dorset. If it was possible to put the clock back, I can think of fewer more pleasant things to do than take a day excursion to Bournemouth after the manner of the one I so enjoyed 40 years ago.

# 5 · INLAND WESSEX
## Cross-Country Blandford to Petworth

There is always a problem in a book of this sort establishing an appropriate dividing line between what to include and what to leave out. It is not only a question of suitable material, but also one of geographic limitations — how far inland from the coast should be admissible to avoid "a bridge too far"? In the final analysis any judgment is bound to be arbitrary, so I must ask readers' indulgence for what has been selected for this chapter.

The origins of the Somerset & Dorset system in the south can be traced to the opening of a ten and-a-quarter mile branch from Wimborne Minster to Blandford Forum on 1 November, 1860. Built to the same gauge as the Southampton and Dorchester line, it was worked by the LSWR from the beginning. This is not the place to reiterate the fascinating history of the Somerset & Dorset, but Blandford remained the most important station on the line south of Templecombe Junction throughout its existence. This importance was emphasised when the cut-off link from Bailey Gate to Broadstone Junction was built in the mid-1880s, for only local services and freight continued to use the old line to Wimborne while through trains for the coast were able to avoid a time-consuming reversal there and travel direct to Bournemouth. In fact, Somerset & Dorset passenger trains ceased running to Wimborne at all from 11 July, 1920; through freight was discontinued from 17 June, 1933, though the line from Corfe Mullen Junction remained in use as a siding for part of its

length until 1959 and the rusting single track lay disused for some years after that.

Although Blandford straddled the same River Stour that flowed into the western waters of the Solent at Christchurch, it was some time before I came to know it moderately well. Being several miles inland it was not on the purely coastal route, nor on the main road arteries to the West such as the A30 or A303, but rather an intersection on diagonals connecting Salisbury with Dorchester or Poole with Sherborne or Shaftesbury. Without one's own transport it was not easily accessible from Fareham in a day, but the periodic visits to Upper Parkstone nearly always resulted in an outing over the Somerset & Dorset! I have been lucky enough to ride behind a Stanier 'Black Five' 4-6-0 on the Up "Pines Express", and an assortment of older or smaller Somerset & Dorset motive power on stopping trains to Templecombe — 2P 4-4-0, 2MT 'Mickey Mouse' 2-6-2T or 4F 'Armstrong' 0-6-0 — as well as some of the BR Standard designs drafted in during the final years. But perhaps the most poignant moment of all was during the afternoon of Saturday, 8 September, 1962. That summer I had been working with a firm of solicitors in Southbourne, a temporary position while one of the partners was abroad, living in digs at Barton-on-Sea after a few weeks at the YMCA in Bournemouth itself. It permitted closer acquaintance with the Somerset & Dorset line than had been possible hither to — which was just as well, once it

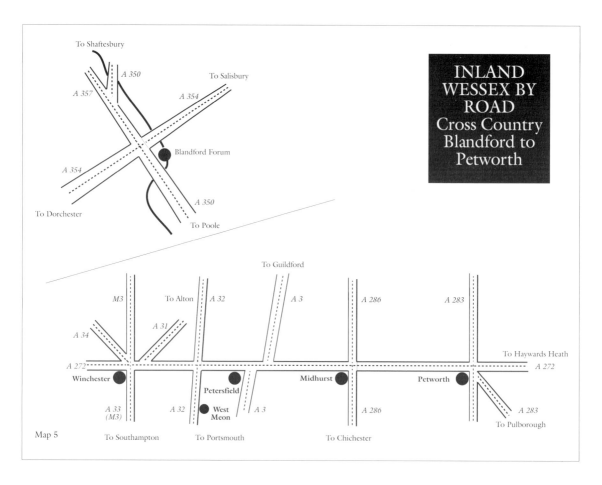

To Shaftesbury

*A 350*

To Salisbury

*A 357*

*A 354*

Blandford Forum

*A 354*

To Dorchester

*A 350*

To Poole

To Guildford

M3    To Alton    *A 32*    *A 3*    *A 286*    *A 283*

*A 34*

*A 31*

To Haywards Heath

*A 272*                                                   *A 272*

Winchester           Midhurst         Petworth

Petersfield

*A 33*      *A 32*    West    *A 3*      *A 286*      *A 283*
*(M3)*              Meon

To Pulborough

Map 5       To Southampton       To Portsmouth       To Chichester

**INLAND WESSEX BY ROAD**
**Cross Country Blandford to Petworth**

*Saturday at Blandford Forum. One of the handsome camel-back Bristol LL6Bs, among the last half-cab coaches ordered from Duple by Royal Blue, loads for Ilfracombe opposite the Crown Hotel on 8 September, 1962. No. 1276 (LTA 864) seated 37 passengers and was operated for 13 years on express duties. A livery change, with a cream roof instead of blue, occurred towards the end of its working life. Note the autovac beside the bonnet.*

became known that the '62 season was to be the last for through summer holiday trains. It also meant that the "Pines Express" would be diverted away from the Somerset & Dorset and the whole 71 (and-a-half) miles from Bath to Bournemouth reduced to a mere branch line. So, after a sandwich lunch at Corfe Mullen Junction watching Down trains entering the single track section to Broadstone, I drove my little Austin 7 north-west along the A350 to Blandford. Parking was not as difficult in 1962 as it is today, so the black 'Ruby' was left unobtrusively outside the railway station in Oakfield Street. As I had allowed plenty of time, I wandered around some of the shops (early closing was on Wednesdays) while waiting for the last Down "Pines". As luck would have it, a Royal Blue coach on Associated Motorways duty bound for Ilfracombe was loading nearby. It dawned on me that a photograph of one of the last examples of a Bristol 'LL6B' still active with its original operator might not come amiss, so I took two pictures to finish up the film before putting a fresh one into the Zeiss camera ready for that train. Walking back to the station, I quickened my step for I didn't want to be late today of all days!

A small group of onlookers gathered soon after 5 pm on the Down platform. They were not 'enthusiasts', just ordinary local people come to see the train that had been the very spirit of the Somerset & Dorset pass by for the last time. On Saturdays the "Pines" ran a little later from Bath than on weekdays, although it contrived to set out from Manchester five minutes earlier — such was the weekend congestion on holiday routes in summer! A distant whistle was heard, then after a minute or two a big engine nosed under the little girder bridge and drifted gently into the platform. A wreath partly obscured the smokebox number, but there was no mistaking "Evening Star".

Doyen of the 9F 2-10-0s, no. 92220 had been built at Swindon just over two years before, the final steam locomotive for the nationalised railway and much in demand for special duties. It had already worked for the last Up "Pines" that day, so the men at Bath Motive Power Depot (82F — formerly 71G) must have turned the engine round pretty quickly — coaling, watering, lubricating —to manage the second leg. It didn't hoot, like either the Stanier or BR 5MT 4-6-0s, but its piercing whistle lingered loud and long before the ten driving wheels began to move in unison. With a brace of Gresley carriages behind the tender, it was a cosmopolitan assortment of stock that rattled over the points beyond the platform. As the 9Fs deep exhaust receded into the distance, the quivering of signal wires followed by a solid 'clunk' confirmed the final "Pines Express" had gone; each of us left Blandford with a heavy heart.

Though I am sure that many readers will have their own tales to tell of other towns and villages across inland Wessex, I hope no one will mind if this narrative centres upon Petersfield. Romsey, Winchester and Alton each have some special claim to fame, but lack of space compels one to be selective — and I did spend seven very formative years at Churcher's College. The old market town of Petersfield nestles in the lea of the South Downs, the twin escarpments of Butser and War Down being high enough to ensure ample rainfall immediately to the north of them. I went to school there at the age of eleven, boarding for nine months of the year, which was sufficiently long to make certain that something of the local flavour rubbed off on me.

Hardly had the family moved from Hilsea to Catisfield, it seemed, than I was packed off to boarding school. But Petersfield, being a natural crossroads for travellers, had quite a

*The quintessential local train over the Somerset & Dorset: class 2P 4-4-0 no. 40564 and Maunsell three-coach set 395 form the 5.30 pm from Bournemouth West to Templecombe on 4 June, 1960. The distinctive two-lamp headcode on a Fowler locomotive at the head of Southern rolling stock was a combination of long standing on this line. 40564, built in 1928, was coasting into Creekmoor Halt before attending to the serious business of a standing start on the 1 in 75 of Broadstone Bank with a four-coupled engine!*

*To mark the last Pines Express over the Somerset & Dorset, class 9F 2-10-0 no. 92220 Evening Star was rostered for the Down train on Saturday, 8 September, 1962. In smart Brunswick Green paintwork, and with a wreath on the smokebox, the huge locomotive gave tongue as it drew out of Blandford on the final leg of the journey from Manchester (London Road) to Bournemouth West.*

*Outside the administration block of Eastleigh MPD (71A) class 0395 0-6-0 no. 30566 hissed happily after having its fire raked and surplus ash thrown out. Designed by William Adams for the LSWR in the 1880s, this remarkable survivor of the Victorian Age was still in regular use for light shunting and pick-up goods work when pictured on 29 December, 1956. Next to it was 30757 Earl of Mount Edgcumbe.*

lot to offer in the way of transport. At first I missed the freedom to come and go as I pleased — which I had taken for granted until then — but there were two occasions each week when it was possible to 'escape', lawfully. On Friday afternoon, after the final lesson, boarders were allowed to visit the town for shopping but, like Cinderella, one had to be back for roll-call just before tea at 5 pm. Without a bicycle (at first) this meant much of the precious hour was spent merely in transit to or from the shops, some of which were more than a mile from the school. There were three possible ways of tackling the problem in one's first year: develop an athletic constitution, catch any available bus or, in extremis, be late back! I tried all three — then pleaded for a bicycle. Before my wish could be granted (first year boarders were not allowed bikes, for some obscure reason), I did make use of the buses. On occasion, if one was lucky, the fare could be 'saved' by blending into the mass of day boys, most of whom had

season tickets, but it was much more difficult when coming back from the town as one might be the only pupil travelling that way. Also, departures seemed to be set to allow too little time for shopping or to meet the roll-call deadline. The best compromise, funds permitting, was to catch the Aldershot & District bus into Petersfield and then return independently "at best speed". While this not infrequently resulted in a hot, sweaty, dishevelled arrival in the roll-call queue, most pre-teenage youngsters are not too particular about their appearance. Of rather more interest was the East Lancs-bodied Dennis 'Lance', due outside the College gates on the 24 service from Guildford via Hindhead at just after the final bell! I didn't appreciate then that the 'CCG' series had mostly been rebodied and had the reliable 5-cylinder Gardner diesel engine found in so many of Hants & Dorset's older Bristol buses (as well as in a lot of Southdown's utility Guys), but I had a lot to learn! The lowbridge body-

An intriguing line-up of Leyland Titan double-deckers outside Eastleigh railway station in about 1944. On the far left is TD2 no. M154 (LJ 7094) of 1933, in the middle is TD1 no. E362 (OW 485) of 1931 with TD2 no. G136 (LJ 5018) of 1932 on the right. Their lowbridge bodies were by Brush, Leyland and Beadle, respectively, the last being rebodied in 1943 and painted grey. G136 was later allocated to Woolston garage and often appeared in Fareham on service 80. All were equipped with the Gardner 5LW diesel engine during the late-1930s to improve fuel economy

A rural bus service was operated for a number of years by Little Wonder between Alresford and Petersfield. One of the vehicles used was a Bedford 'OB' with bodywork by Plaxton — JX 9673 originated in Halifax in the early months of 1947 before migrating south at some later date. This Fifties view portrays the Little Wonder stand in Broad Street, Alresford. Services were also operated between Petersfield and Buriton. (Alan Lambert)

Sunday in Petersfield Square could produce unexpected sights! An elderly Southdown vehicle had arrived with a visiting rugby team from Sussex, while the H & D coach (right) was on an excursion to the Meon Valley and Southsea. The Harrington-bodied Leyland Tiger TS4 no. 1076 (UF 9776) started life in 1933, being fitted with a full-length band-box for luggage or instruments; at some stage it was modified with a Coventry style radiator and 8.6 litre diesel engine. The Bristol L6B, new in 1948/9 with stylish Dutfield coachwork of half-canopy design, at first numbered TC 824 in the Hants & Dorset fleet — when this picture was taken in 1951 it had been renumbered 653 (HRU 451) but retained the ornate livery.

*Warren's Altonian coaches in the post-war period comprised an assortment of Bedfords plus a brace of Tilling-Stevens. The company also had a fleet of trucks and, as the combined total of vehicles exceeded the available yard's capacity, off-street parking for the older coaches was often in Alton's car parks. This late-Sixties picture shows two Duple-bodied Bedford coaches plus GOU 586/732. These Tilling-Stevens had Gardner 6LW engines and Scottish Aviation bodies of 1948 vintage.*

work was interesting, because the East Lancs double-deckers that Southdown had fitted to a number of prewar Leylands were of highbridge construction. The Dennis 'Lance' coasted down Ramshill, then squeezed under the railway bridge at the bottom before turning left into College Street — where the original Churcher's building was used by the local authority. As the driver passed the Red Lion (with Wadham's Garage and small showrooms opposite), he would put his arm out of the cab window to indicate the bus was about to turn right by the War Memorial into High Street, pulling up by the girls' High School. The next stop was in the centre, the best place for a limited degree of shopping (ration books were still in vogue) and

the chance of a quick browse in Childs' book-shop located at 1, The Square.

As only the foolhardy delayed much after 4.35 pm before setting off back to the College at a brisk pace, there was little opportunity to see the 'Middy' up at the railway station. This could be done at leisure on Sundays — though even that opportunity ceased after the 1950/1 coal shortage, following which all services were 'rationalised' and those on Sunday curtailed altogether. Still, for my first couple of years there it was a good time to see the little branch train for Midhurst and Pulborough. Boarders were allowed out after lunch, ostensibly to go walking or cycling for recreation in the truly

*As the last public passenger train ran between Alton and Fareham on Saturday, 5 February, the replacement bus service began operation the following day. A sparkling Leyland Titan PD2 with full lining-out and informative destination screens (front, side and rear) prepares to leave Alton railway station on the first southbound service to Portsmouth (Theatre Royal) at 10.13 am on Sunday, 6 February, 1955. No. 389 (JCD 89) was an all-Leyland highbridge model purchased in 1948, giving an indication of the high standard Southdown maintained for so many years — note the chrome radiator. (Alan Lambert)*

unspoiled countryside of East Hampshire and West Sussex, within very easy reach of school. Happily, the Southern Railway had set a precedent by timetabling the 12.33 pm from Pulborough to reach Petersfield by 1.28 pm, after which it occupied the bay platform opposite the signal box for the best part of a couple of hours. One became mesmerised by the uneven tempo of the Westinghouse pump, which was mounted on the right hand side of the smokebox on a Drummond M7, or immediately in front of the entrance to the cam on a 'Brighton' four-coupled tank such as a D1 0-4-2T or D3 0-4-4T. Nearly always the engine on the 'Middy' ran chimney-first from Petersfield, so the pump was on the platform side. I can recall watching the crew preparing their locomotive for departure, raking out the ash and washing down the footplate, oiling the hundred and one moving parts or making up the fire, with the irregular panting of the pump

providing a sort of rhythmic bass for all this activity. Then, while the tanks were being filled with water from the crane beside Tilmore Bridge, I and any of my school friends would scuttle off along the A272 road past the Southdown Bus Garage to Ramshill Bridge. Turning right into Love Lane, which ran parallel with the track for a short distance in the direction of the playing fields, there was a footpath up the embankment and over the railway at Moggs Mede. At this point one could lawfully stand beside the line and watch the train pass on its way to Midhurst and Pulborough, before turning back slowly along Love Lane to the College. The exertions of the ancient tank engine could be heard soon after it left the platform at 3.19 pm and, as we stood waiting to wave our caps when it passed, perhaps the driver would give an acknowledgement on the shrill whistle. Sometimes one might retrieve a much-enlarged farthing or halfpenny after the train had puffed out of sight.

Let us end this cross-country ramble in West Sussex. In a sense we have followed the A272 across the county boundary from Winchester and Petersfield to Midhurst and Petworth, running from west to east parallel with the coast but roughly 15-20 miles inland. Because of its importance one finds there is a market town at every north-south intersection. The pity is no railway runs cross-country

*Shunting operations in Bishop's Waltham goods yard during the final weeks before closure: class 2MT 2-6-2T no. 41214 has assembled its train on 1 March, 1962, and is preparing the return to the station before continuing to Botley. Freight facilities were withdrawn after 27 April that year and a road now runs along the old trackbed at this point; both station and goods shed were demolished.*

this far from London to carry the heavier freight; some lines were built in the 19th century, but they did not form a complete network to be viable in a more competitive world. The branch from Petersfield to Midhurst — The 'Middy' — was opened by the LSWR on 1 September, 1864, but after 90 years as a country backwater the closure notices were posted and all traffic was suspended from 7 February, 1955. From Midhurst to Petworth and Pulborough as well as southwards to Lavant and Chichester the LBSCR was responsible for Sussex branch activities; the former line was completed on 15 October, 1866, and the latter on 11 July, 1881. The Southern Railway inherited all these rural routes on 1 January, 1923, and soon upgraded the Bepton Road bridge at Midhurst to enable passenger trains to use the 1881 ex-LBSCR station, rather than people having to walk the half-a-mile from the former LSWR terminus at Midhurst Common

if they wanted a connecting service.

The new arrangements came into force on 12 July, 1925, following which Midhurst Common station closed; the goods sidings continued in use even after passenger services were withdrawn. The line south of Midhurst became freight-only from 6 July, 1935. An unfortunate washout of a culvert, following heavy rainfall, caused a derailment on 19 November, 1951, to the Up goods from Chichester, north of Cocking. The line was never reinstated, freight facilities being withdrawn from Cocking and Singleton after 28 August, 1953, with just Lavant remaining open (3·25 miles from Chichester) to become a railhead for local sugar-beet traffic until January 1970. Midhurst lost its goods trains some nine and-a-half years after the passenger services were suspended (from 7 February, 1955), closing completely on 16 October, 1964. Petworth

*( Continued on page 89 )*

The matching arc-roofed canopies of Shawford (for Twyford) provide the setting for rebuilt 'Battle of Britain' 4-6-2 no. 34085 '501 Squadron' belting through with an Up boat train from Southampton Docks to Waterloo on 27 July, 1962; Pullman cars are included in the rake of assorted stock. Sadly, the station has been much altered and lost its architectural charm in the process.

One of the things to look out for at Winchester (City) was a diminutive tank engine, shunting. As late as 1963 it might still be one of Adams' 'B4' 0-4-0Ts, originally intended for Southampton Docks, because the curvature of the Up side goods yard was so sharp that only a short wheelbase machine could cope. On 29 October, 1962, no. 30096 was performing with gusto — a car park now occupies this site.

A rare sight over the Mid-Hants: owing to engineering works on the main line around Basingstoke, certain services were re-routed 'over the Alps'. On Sunday 8 January, 1961, the Down Bournemouth Belle was affected! Rebuilt Merchant Navy 4-6-2 no. 35018 British India Line had the assistance of 'U' 2-6-0 no. 31628 when this prestige train swept through Ropley, the Pullmans making a brave sight on a single-track branch normally the preserve of dull, diesel multiple units. Nearly 30 years later, British India Line is at Ropley once more, under restoration to full working order after being salvaged from Barry scrapyard — perhaps we shall see this scene re-enacted in the 1990s?

Moment of departure: the branch train to Midhurst stands in the bay platform opposite the signal box at Petersfield, just to the north of the level crossing, as the guard and station foreman wait for the driver to look back from the footplate. The notice board on the left of the picture advises passengers to 'Cross the road for main line trains' and warns of road traffic on the A272. Carriage S 6429 S was the driving trailer brake composite in push-pull set 653. (C. White)

Epitome of a rural railway: class M7 0-4-4T no. 30049 of Horsham MPD (75D) pauses for a moment at Elsted with a single push-pull carriage from Midhurst to Petersfield in the winter of 1954/5. This former LSWR branch line, known affectionately as The Middy, was opened on 1 September, 1864, and closed just over 90 years later. The bridge over the trackbed still remains today. (C. White)

The Chichester to Midhurst pick-up goods was meandering northwards minding its own business on 19 November, 1951, when the track gave way at a culvert near Cocking. Though the crew escaped unhurt, coal from the engine's tender fed the boiler for some time. 32522 remained stuck in its watery grave for several weeks until the floodwater had subsided. Eventually the class C2x Vulcan 0-6-0 was recovered and repaired, but trains ran no more towards Midhurst from the south and Lavant became the railhead for freight. (C. White)

One of the many second-hand vehicles acquired by Basil Williams for his various companies was a former Leicester Corporation Leyland Titan TD4c with MCW highbridge bodywork. New in 1936, it was one of six gearless examples purchased in 1950. After being repainted in Hants & Sussex colours, ABC 183 sometimes helped out on the Liss & District route 1 between Petersfield, Longmoor and Liphook, though it never achieved fleetnames or numbers before withdrawal in 1953. This rare picture was obtained at the top of Ramshill, opposite Churcher's College on a journey to Longmoor in 1952.

The Southdown bus service linking Chichester, Midhurst and Petersfield was the route 60. Because of some low trees and the Ramshill bridge over the A3 road at Petersfield, double-deck buses with sunken gangways (the lowbridge style of bodywork) were used. As no lowbridge vehicles were taken into stock by Southdown after World War II, buses on service 60 tended to be quite elderly. Leyland Titan TD2 no. 957 (UF 9757) was new in June 1933, but its Short Bros. highbridge body was replaced with a utility lowbridge design by Willowbrook in 1944, as displayed in this late-1940s view bound for Petersfield. Note the green-painted radiator. (A.B. Cross)

Rural crumb-catcher: a smart new Bristol RESL with Marshall body filled the narrow roadway through Amberley village on a Horsham to Arundel journey in February 1969. Uneconomic services like this were severely curtailed during the 1970s and 1980s. In traditional Southdown livery, car 219 (KUF 219F) displayed full destination information for service 71 — now just a memory.

*Rural freight with autumnal shadows lengthening, class C2x Vulcan, no. 32549 makes a rousing exit from Petworth on 23 October, 1961, with a trainload of sugar-beet forming the 12.30 pm pick-up goods from Midhurst to Pulborough. For the few remaining Vulcan 0-6-0s this was their Indian summer — by the end of January 1962, all were withdrawn for scrap.*

( Continued from page 85 )

followed suit from 20 May, 1966; within a hundred years the various railways to Midhurst had come and gone.

By the autumn of 1968, while I continued working at Godalming in Surrey, I moved into a small centuries-old cottage in the village of Amberley to start married life. Set in a fold of the Downs, it is a charming place with its wild brooks, church and ruined castle. The railway station, though named after the village, is actually closer to Houghton — but, no doubt like rural dwellers everywhere, the people of Amberley were used to walking. After the end of World War II, Southdown Motor Services extended its Storrington to Thakeham bus service 71 to serve Amberley; indeed, the route at its peak ran between Littlehampton and Horsham, but this had been reduced from a frequent operation to a mere shadow of its former self by 1968.

Like many other Southdown country services, I expect the 71 used to be the preserve of that company's magnificent series of Leyland 'Tiger' saloons with Harrington bodywork, no fewer than 86 of which were added to the fleet between 1935 and 1940. By the time I became acquainted with Amberley, the route was served by a modern Bristol 'RESL' with neat Marshall 45-seat body, a type introduced only that year. The unusual feature about these buses, which looked very well in traditional Southdown colours, was a manual gearbox coupled to the Gardner diesel engine mounted at the rear; later versions had the more usual semi-automatic arrangement. But if the rear-engined single-decker was the latest thing (if not the best!) since sliced bread, Petworth still maintained a strong tradition from times past. With narrow streets and a quaint one-way system, it seemed steeped in history that was reluctant to admit the presence of motorised

transport. Southdown had managed to squeeze a small depot into an awkward site on the Pulborough road, which may explain why crew-operated double-deckers were still based there for the 22 service in 1968 — a bus reversing in or out of that depot completely blocked the main A283 and must have been a hazard even with the help of a conductor. From its zenith between 1955 and 1960, when it had operated from Brighton right through to Petersfield, the 22 service had been cut back first to Midhurst and then to Petworth where it terminated in the Square. Handsome, if dated, Leyland 'Titan' PD2/12s were the mainstay of this cross-country route: over the years there had been examples with bodywork by Leyland, Northern Counties, Park Royal, Beadle and East Lancs, all with half-cabs and rear loading with platform doors. Alternate journeys between Fittleworth and Petworth were diverted through Byworth village, but over the rest of the route an hourly service was maintained for much of the day. On Fridays only, service 22A provided a link between Petworth, Tillington and Upperton at infrequent intervals, probably to help get the weekend shopping home — but did the inhabitants of tiny Upperton really need a 59-seater for their Christmas and New Year purchases?

*All along the A272, the country towns were important market and shopping centres where various operator's bus services met. Aldershot & District routes met those of Southdown at Petersfield, Midhurst and Petworth. Some skill was required to negotiate narrow streets and tight corners in these old market towns, as evidenced by Southdown's Leyland Titan PD2 no. 780 (RUF 180) on service 161 at Petworth on 27 December, 1968. A Beadle 59-seat body was fitted.*

# 6 · HAVANT TO HAYLING
## By Rail and Road

Between Chichester Harbour and Langstone lie the two islands of Thorney and Hayling. The former established its place in history as a RAF base during World War II, and has been served ever since by buses operated by Mr. Basil Williams — some mention of his Hants & Sussex vehicles was made in connection with Fareham. But to the west of Thorney, lies the much larger island of Hayling, rather like an upside-down T. Indeed, at its western extremity it is less than a quarter-of-a-mile from Portsea Island, being linked by a small ferry boat. But the main access to Hayling has always been from the north — since 1867 two bridges joined the island to the mainland at Langstone, one for the single-line railway from Havant and a toll bridge for foot passengers, driven animals, carts and other road users.

The little train to Hayling had a chequered history in its early days, with the Official Receiver being called in at one stage, but it managed to stay in business, largely thanks to support from the London, Brighton & South Coast Railway until formation of the Southern on 1 January, 1923, when the Hayling line was absorbed into the new conglomerate. Not that very much changed, because the sort of steam locomotive that took over operation of the branch in the 1890s was not only still in charge at the time of the Grouping but remained in use to perform the closing ceremonies on 3 November, 1963! The passenger train improved from uncomfortable four-wheelers of

19th Century ancestry to non-corridor bogie carriages by the late-1920s, but it should also be remembered that the very last train of all contained four non-corridor coaches out of a rake of five...

Hayling had much in common with the Isle of Wight, not least because some of its ancient engines had been shipped back across the Solent in the late-1940s for further service. On the roads — or perhaps I should say 'road', for the B2149 was the only means of getting four-wheeled vehicles on or off the Island — matters did change over the years. The ancient timber toll bridge restricted the type of bus that could be used owing to the weight limit imposed, for it had been constructed in a different age without thought for the 20th Century horseless carriage. As the 1950s advanced, the weight limit was reduced to conserve the old bridge while a new concrete structure began to rise alongside. This added restriction caused great inconvenience to bus passengers, who were turfed off and obliged to walk across in all weathers, being met by another bus on the far side. In response to the swelling tide of complaints, one small Southdown bus was specially adapted as a stop-gap measure to shuttle at least some passengers over the bridge between the main setting-down and picking-up points on either side, while the new bridge was being finished. Leyland 'Cub' no. 23 (ECD 523) was never the most popular vehicle, especially when all non-essential items had been removed to reduce

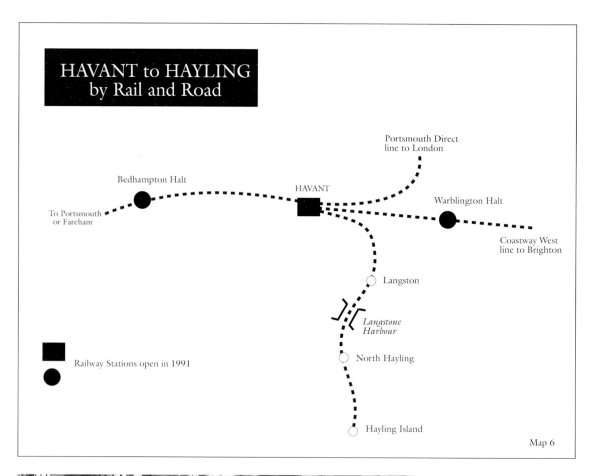

HAVANT to HAYLING
by Rail and Road

Portsmouth Direct
line to London

Bedhampton Halt

HAVANT

Warblington Halt

To Portsmouth
or Fareham

Coastway West
line to Brighton

Langston

Langstone
Harbour

North Hayling

■ Railway Stations open in 1991

Hayling Island

Map 6

*Above : Havant station forecourt on the south side was the best place to wait for a bus for Hayling in summer. Southdown Leyland Cub no. 8 (DUF 8) was setting off on route 47 via Manor Road one sunny afternoon as a couple more small saloons were filling up behind. Points worth noting in this 1950s glimpse are the water crane for branch steam engines (behind the bus stop sign), the deeper than normal destination display unique to no. 8 (all other Cub buses had a 10 inch deep aperture) and the rear-entrance Park Royal body with luggage rack. (D. Clark)*

*Left (page 92) : Despite advancing years, the six forward-control Leyland Cub saloons (nos. 7-12) continued to be active on Hayling Island services until the new bridge at Langstone opened in the autumn of 1956. In this picture taken in about 1953, Cub no. 12 was crossing the main A27 road opposite Havant church, bound for Eastoke while a rebodied Southdown Titan TD5 (161: EUF 161) waited to turn into East Street on the 43A service to Denvilles and Westbourne. (D. Clark)*

weight, but it served until the wooden bridge was finally replaced in 1956. I did not use the bus to reach Hayling after 1952 or thereabouts, so I have no personal experience of the problems that were encountered — it was so much easier to catch the train! Nevertheless, I have very clear recollections of Hayling in high summer during the late-1940s.

At a time when car travel was a luxury for the few and foreign holidays were for the very few, a couple of days by the seaside was as much as most ordinary folk could hope for after the end of the war. A trip to Hayling during the long school break was an exciting prospect. Being a weekday, my father would be at work, so we had to go by bus. From Hilsea that meant one bus as far as Havant, then change on to a smaller machine to reach the golden beaches for which Hayling was justly famous. While food was still very much rationed, sandwiches for lunch never seemed to be in short supply and armed with these and a bottle of lemonade — no ring-pull cans in the Forties — we

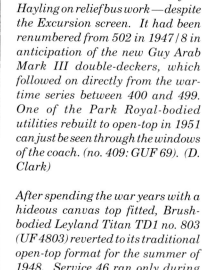

*Helping out at times of pressure, the Leyland Cheetah coaches had centre-entrance bodywork by Park Royal. In the later style of livery with reduced areas of dark green, no. 602 (EUF 502) is on duty at Hayling on relief bus work—despite the Excursion screen. It had been renumbered from 502 in 1947/8 in anticipation of the new Guy Arab Mark III double-deckers, which followed on directly from the wartime series between 400 and 499. One of the Park Royal-bodied utilities rebuilt to open-top in 1951 can just be seen through the windows of the coach. (no. 409: GUF 69). (D. Clark)*

*After spending the war years with a hideous canvas top fitted, Brush-bodied Leyland Titan TD1 no. 803 (UF 4803) reverted to its traditional open-top format for the summer of 1948. Service 46 ran only during the summer between Hayling bus station (later Beachlands) and the Ferry across to Eastney; it was normally provided by one of these antique survivors until the end of the 1950 season. 803 paused at South Hayling railway station whilst in transit to the Ferry, but most passengers seem to be on the lower deck! (D. Clark)*

walked to the end of Military Road. The bus stops for services leaving the City were on the opposite side of the main road, beside the Lido. Any bus for Havant would do; service 31 for Brighton, 43 to Westbourne or 48 for Rowlands Castle and Horndean. Both the 31 and 48 services were double-deckers, but the 43 could often produce one of Southdown's famous '1400s' as an alternative to an oil-engined TD4 or TD5 'decker. From Hilsea the bus went over Northern Road bridge to Cosham, before turning eastwards to the Red Lion. Along the Havant Road past St. Colman's Church, then through Drayton and Farlington in quick succession brought the bus to the

level crossing by Bedhampton Halt. It kept straight ahead over the railway, and we alighted at Havant church.

At first we waited in South Street for a connection to Hayling, but it was not really the best place to queue if the weather was fine and hundreds of other families had the same destination in mind. After seeing the first few buses go past without stopping, already full-up, we trudged along North Street towards the station where the Hayling services began. Every bus was a single-decker; three varieties of Leyland 'Cub', a centre-entrance Dennis 'Falcon' and — if one was lucky — an example or two of the Leyland 'Cheetah'. The last type together with the coach version of the 'Cub' sported a sun-

*Winter finale: in the arctic conditions that prevailed during the first weeks of 1963, class A1x 0-6-0T no. 32661 keeps on the boil with the Hayling branch train at Havant station. Staff have cleared the thick snow from the platform where the ancient locomotive and its two carriages normally stand, partly for safety reasons and also to prevent the coach interiors becoming too wet. A spark arrester was hardly necessary in such conditions.*

*Hayling high summer: class A1x 0-6-0T no. 32646 drifts into North Hayling Halt with the 4.35 pm from Havant to Hayling Island service on 18 June, 1961. Terriers were permitted to take up to four coaches unaided, but with the heavier stock drafted in during the late-1950s any more than three was a bit of a struggle for an octogenarian. 32646 had spent many years in the Isle of Wight before returning to the mainland in 1949 — now preserved in working order, it has crossed the Solent once again to be based at Haven Street.*

roof, an inspired idea for hot summer days that made the long delays more bearable than if one was cooped up in an overcrowded bus with too little ventilation. Outside the railway station stretched a long queue of hopeful passengers waiting for any variation on the 47 theme that would take them, eventually, to Beachlands and within sight of that marvellous, safe, sandy shore. It was a complete lottery which type of bus one travelled on — as each turned round in the station forecourt and pulled up at the stop, a milling throng pressed forward but only the first 30 or so would be lucky enough to get on board. Even then, no more than 26 would actually get seats (less still if the vehicle was a coach) while the remainder had to stand! With a faint whiff of petrol, the lightweight machine (whether Leyland or Dennis) would be started

*What a way to go...  The empty stock for the very last train to Hayling Island was brought up the main line from Fratton to Havant behind the two original Terriers built for the LBSCR in 1872, nos. 32670 and 32636. Gleaming in the late autumn sunshine, their five-coach train comprised more BR-built non-corridors and a Maunsell brake composite — the whole entourage was recorded for posterity approaching Bedhampton Halt on Sunday, 3 November, 1963.  R.I.P.*

again, idling for a few moments before the driver let in the clutch and set off southwards at what seemed like break-neck speed. In such crowded conditions it was too much to expect to get my favoured seat immediately behind the driver on the offside, where it was possible to watch both the speedometer and the road ahead.  On the 20-seater 'Cubs' (both buses and coaches) the passengers were in with the

driver and the instruments were placed in the centre of the dashboard, whereas with the half-cab forward-control vehicles the driver was separated by a bulkhead in the usual way.

After crossing the A27 road by Havant church the route was shaded for a while.  Let us suppose circumstance had smiled upon our group of patient travellers, and 24 of us had

*On the last day of normal service, class A1x 0-6-0T no. 32650 clears its tubes and bustles along the single track towards North Hayling with the 11.35 am from Havant. On the left of the picture the timber viaduct can be clearly seen at low tide, while on the right the modern road bridge appears spindly by comparison. Signal posts shorn of their fittings tell their own tale...*

managed to get seats aboard one of the eleven Park Royal coach-bodied Leyland 'Cheetahs' at Havant, so that the open sunroof let in ample quantities of fresh air and granted most passengers the pleasure of an uninterrupted view — upwards! The 'Cheetah' was an intermediate size of coach with a lively 6-cylinder petrol engine; Southdown's examples were intended for both excursion work and express duties between London and Hayling Island, but in peak season it was quite normal for them to help out on bus services as well. I cannot adequately describe in mere words the subtle sounds and sensations produced by a

ride in a petrol-engined coach, but it was always a stimulating experience. The hiss of the carburettor harnessed to the scream of the transmission in the indirect gears never failed to make one's pulse beat quicker, but as the coach approached Langstone any chance of speed was lost as vehicles queued helplessly, first for the railway level crossing and then for the toll bridge. Once clear of that rickety structure, there were several possible routes ahead, via Northney, Gable Head or Eastoke, but the objective was always Beachlands Bus Station. Even as one stepped off there was the gritty feel of sand underfoot, whipped up in fine particles by the wind and deposited along the sea front. But before leaving the bus station to revel in the simple pleasures of that beach, another petrol-engined vehicle on service 46 might swing round the corner. This was the preserve of one of the 1929-built open-top Leyland 'Titan' TD1s, the only route to be worked by a double-decker on Hayling before the new bridge enabled buses of all kinds to penetrate where few had gone before. The Brush-bodied TD1s had outlived many more modern covered-top buses by being adapted during the war with a hideous canvas roof, and all 23 gave at least a score of years' loyal service. Most were based at Hilsea and at Brighton, with one or two of the former's allocation being out-stationed on Hayling throughout the season each summer, restored to their primeval state — and very popular on the 46 to and from the ferry. Their unladen weight of around 6 tons allowed them to be driven empty across the toll bridge, but once there the veterans' activities were confined to the 46 route wholly on Hayling Island. Their days on scheduled service came to an end with the 1951 season, after which they were replaced by rebuilt utility Guys — the first regular diesels on Hayling — but for some years a handful lingered on tree-lopping duties all over the Southdown empire; by great good fortune one has survived to this day.

The 46 route passed by the railway terminus at South Hayling, and often provided a useful connection for passengers bound for Beachlands. In later years the service was renumbered 149, but understandably it did not run between the end of September and the start of the following summer season, for Hayling can be inhospitable for visitors in the cold or the wet. I remember once when the weather took a turn for the worse; it had started off as a hot sultry day when we wanted nothing more than to cool off in the shallow water of low tide. Soon after midday a storm blew up, we hurriedly changed and headed for the bus stop. As the wind whipped up the sand we sought any form of shelter, shivering in the unforeseen squall in the lee of a battered fence, waiting for a bus — any bus — to take us back to Havant. Others were also cowering from the fury of the elements, so it was a soggy crowd of people that emerged from various hiding places to head for home when an empty bus drew up. It was one of the half-dozen little Leyland 'Cub' buses to have 26-seater rear-entrance bodywork by Park Royal (numbered 7-12). They spent nearly all their lives on Hayling and, to my mind, were among the nicest buses it was ever my privilege to ride on. Certainly, nothing could have been more welcome that stormy summer day as we rattled along the narrow roads, back across the toll bridge to get off at Havant church. As it accelerated away over the crossroads towards the railway station, I was conscious of the useful destination indicator below the rear window — so long a feature of Southdown vehicles and something that has almost entirely disappeared with the passing of the years.

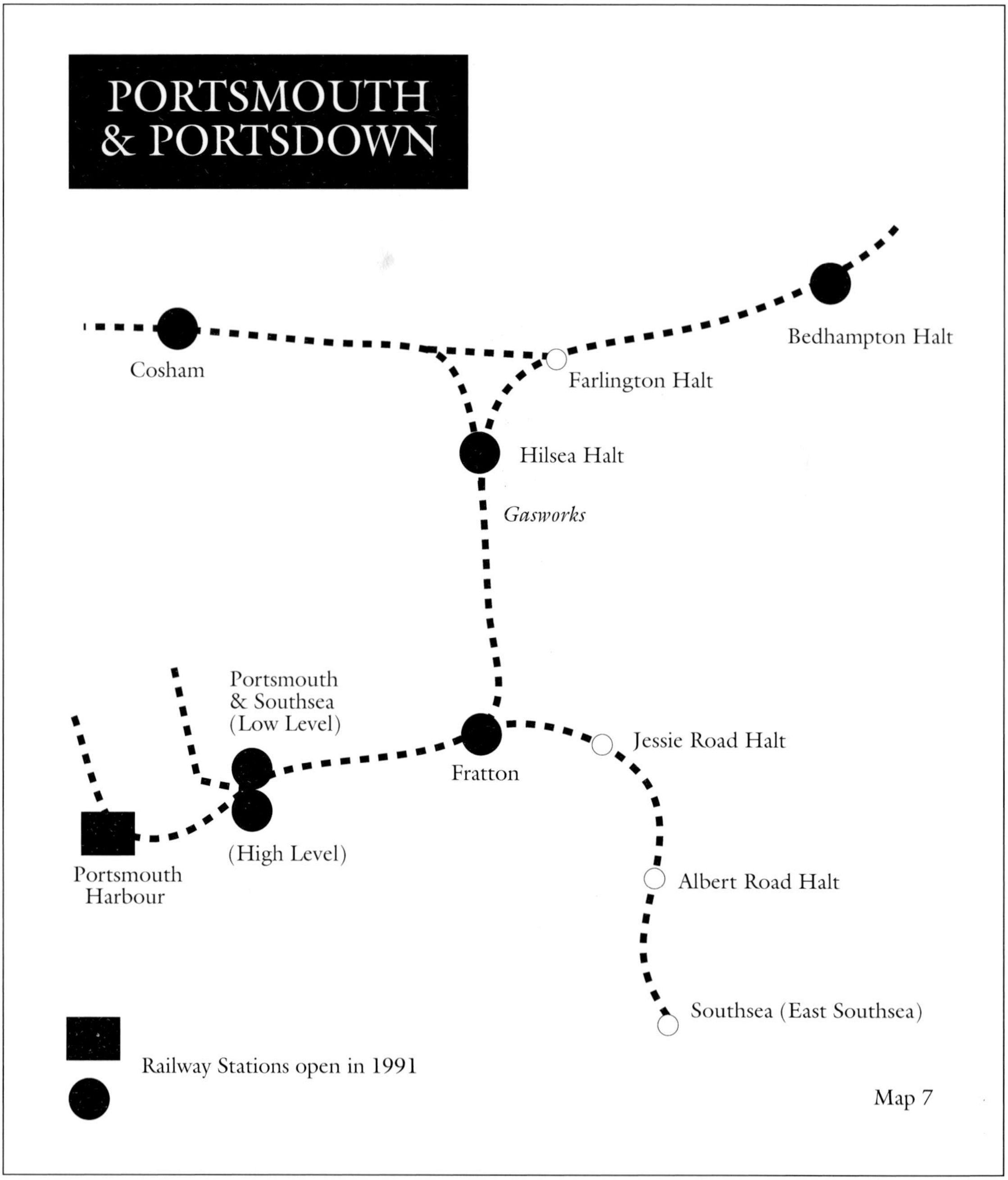

# PORTSMOUTH & PORTSDOWN

Cosham

Bedhampton Halt

Farlington Halt

Hilsea Halt

*Gasworks*

Portsmouth
& Southsea
(Low Level)

Jessie Road Halt

Fratton

Portsmouth
Harbour

(High Level)

Albert Road Halt

Southsea (East Southsea)

Railway Stations open in 1991

Map 7

# 7 · PORTSMOUTH
## *And Portsdown*

While the London & South Western Railway sought to serve the needs of Portsmouth by building a branch line from its route to Southampton in 1841, it terminated on the opposite side of the Harbour in Gosport. This allowed the rival London, Brighton & South Coast concern to be the first to breach the ramparts at Hilsea by extending the railway from Chichester and Havant into the heart of Portsmouth on 14 June, 1847. In under 15 months the LSWR replied by linking Fareham, Portchester and Cosham to the LBSCR route at Farlington and Portcreek Junctions, thus enabling through services to be operated from London (Nine Elms) to Portsmouth via Winchester. Anyone intending to sail to the Isle of Wight was expected to take the train for Gosport and cross the Harbour by launch, or take a train by either LSWR or LBSCR route to Portsmouth and then make their own way to the packet boat at Southsea (Clarence Pier). The Stokes Bay branch line of 1863 offered another alternative, but from 15 May, 1865, the Landport and Southsea Tramway Company inaugurated a street tramway from Portsmouth station that was tailor-made for railway travellers wanting to take passage to the Island. This was the beginning of the trams on the South Coast; an important milestone, since it preceded the passing of the Tramways Act of 1870.

The Portsmouth Street Tramways Company came into being in 1873, just a year after the holding company for the whole Provincial group was founded (the Provincial Tramways Company Limited). Within five years the holding company was able to acquire all the other local tramway companies then operating, but new developments were occurring all the time and it was 1892 before Provincial had complete control on the island of Portsea. In the meantime two further extensions had taken place on the railway; the most important of these was the joint LSWR and LBSCR line to Portsmouth Harbour, including a new steamer berth for packet boats to the Isle of Wight and a high-level addition to the former terminus (in order to avoid crossing Commercial Road on the level), plus a new link to the Dockyard by way of an elevated route to South Railway Jetty on Watering Island. This incorporated a swing bridge and was generally used by special passenger trains, normal goods traffic for the Dockyard being routed over the original line via Edinburgh Road level crossing and Unicorn Gate. The Portsmouth Harbour extension and associated works came into use on 2 October 1876. The other line to be built was from Fratton to Southsea, a mere one-and-a-quarter miles, opened on 1 July, 1885; the terminus in Granada Road was renamed East Southsea in 1896. The Southsea branch had a short life, just 29 years, but it has earned its place in history; operated by each of the two main line companies (LBSCR and LSWR) on alternate years, from 1903 a new design of train was put into service especially to try to compete with urban tramways. A product of the fertile mind of Dugald Drummond, then

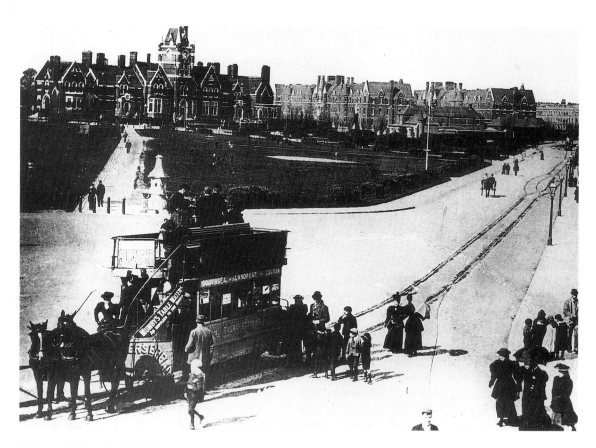

*This was Victorian life in Portsmouth before the Age of the motor car. In the foreground can be seen one of the many horse trams, which has just arrived at the Clarence Pier terminus — the original route of the Landport and Southsea Tramway opened in 1865. Beyond Pembroke Gardens stands Clarence Barracks, with Victoria Barracks to the right. The fashions of the day and the many advertisements on the tramcar summon up the spirit of Southsea 100 years ago. (The News, Portsmouth)*

Locomotive Superintendent of the South Western, his quaint steam railmotor design was copied and enlarged by the Great Western so that it proliferated to most parts of that vast empire until the mid-1930s, two decades after the first two prototypes had ceased shuttling up and down between Fratton and East Southsea.

The reason for the development of steam railmotors to provide cheaper travel over short

distances was not hard to find. By the 1890s the horse trams had spread over much of Portsmouth, and the next step was clearly electrification of the entire system. It was at this point that the Town Council began to consider either acquiring an interest in or purchasing the whole concern, as it was entitled to do under the Tramways Act. Special terms would be needed to cover the section from what is now Portsmouth & Southsea station (the railway terminus until 1876) to

*Edinburgh Road level crossing: class E1 0-6-0T no. 32694 brings the 1.57 pm Fratton Yard to Portsmouth Dockyard freight down from the High Level station past Victoria Park on 20 April, 1956. This was the original route into H M Dockyard, the single line passing round the back of the Post Office and Portsmouth & Sunderland Newspapers before running parallel with Unicorn Road to Unicorn Gate. This short branch was very difficult to photograph as it ran between high brick walls from Edinburgh Road to Unicorn Gate.*

Clarence Pier, since it had been established before the 1870 Act came into force, and the extension beyond the Borough boundary at the Green Posts public house at Hilsea. Full details of all the negotiations leading up to the sale of the tramways to Portsmouth Corporation were described by S.E. Harrison in his book published in 1955. After some dispute over the precise terms of the agreement, the tramcars and routes were handed over to the Corporation at midnight on 31 December 1900 — but there was still argument about the price to be paid. After arbitration, this was finally settled at £185,633. In the meantime, anticipating that 'municipalisation' would take place sooner or later, Provincial had ideas for extending its influence northwards from Cosham. There had been a proposal as long ago as 1885 for a horse-tramway to The George at the top of Portsdown Hill and then on to Waterlooville, but horse buses were used instead; from July 1896 these were extended to Horndean and

became an hourly service in summer. A new Provincial subsidiary, the Hampshire Light Railways (Electric) Company Limited, was incorporated on 17 May, 1897, to further the aim of a tramway out to Horndean, which would be beyond the reach of Portsmouth Corporation. A Light Railway Order was granted for the line's construction on 2 September, 1898, and this was begun in earnest during January 1902 by Dick Kerr & Company Limited, adopting the standard tramway gauge of 4 ft. 7·75 inches to enable through running to take place at some future time. The Portsdown & Horndean Light Railway began operation on 2 March, 1903 from just to the south of the LSWR at Cosham, ascending Portsdown Hill on reserved track before becoming a street tramway near The George. It continued in the centre of the road through Purbrook as far as Waterlooville, after which it ran along the verge on the eastern side to Horndean. While plans were mooted to extend the line down the

*Soon after the opening of the Portsdown & Horndean Light Railway in 1903 this was the scene at the tramway junction at Cosham. The tracks in the foreground belonged to Portsmouth Corporation. In their smart Emerald Green and Cream livery, the Light Railway cars all show Horndean — from left to right they were numbered 7, 16 and 1. An Inspector stands outside the meter house, while a group of slot machines provides amusement for waiting passengers.*

hill into the village, and even on to Petersfield, these never materialised; the northern terminal remained opposite the Good Intent throughout the Light Railway's existence.

My grandfather, John Fereday Glenn, was Manager and Engineer of the Light Railway from its inception until he retired on 31 March, 1924 — it was his name that was carried on the rocker panels on either flank of each tramcar — and Provincial Tramways'

notepaper of around the turn of the century shows both John Glenn (my great-grandfather) and his son to have their local office in Magdala Road, Cosham; the telephone number was Cosham 3!

The fact that the tramway ran for more than thirty years, carrying the Royal Mail for all the rural communities 'over the hill' until closure on 9 January, 1935, and opening up the Portsmouth road (A3) through Purbrook,

Waterlooville and Cowplain as far as Horndean, is highly significant in terms of local history. Older residents around Portsmouth and Portsdown still remember the 'green cars' with great affection, and fondly recall riding up and down the Hill or enjoying family picnics out in the woods beyond Cowplain. The system was bought out by Southdown, which had inherited the bus route following acquisition of the Southsea Tourist Company in 1925. From 1930 Southdown had been able to put to work covered-top Leyland 'Titan' TD1 double-deckers, equipped with sunroof for use in fine weather, thus giving travellers the best of both worlds — undoubtedly, the open-top trams were fine for warm summer days but nowhere near so attractive on cold, frosty winter mornings. Probably more modern vehicles would have been built had Portsmouth Corporation not decided to abandon its own tram system in favour of trolley and motor buses — the final tramcar in the City (as it had become in 1927) ran to Eastney depot on 10 November 1936 — and so jeopardised the through running between Horndean and Southsea that was so vital. There had been petty disagreements in the early days of the Light Railway over the cost of electricity and the use by Corporation cars of the Portsdown Hill section, but after the end of World War I there was growing co-operation between the two, culminating in through running by Light Railway cars from 1 August, 1924, into Portsmouth. This held out the prospect of competing on more equal terms with bus companies, like Southsea Tourist, who had been able to offer a service that avoided having to change at Cosham. But the Light Railway was prevented from establishing a link via Portchester with the other local Provincial subsidiary, the Gosport & Fareham Tramways, by the intransigence of the LSWR during the boom period preceding World War I; had that connecting line been constructed, one can only speculate whether it would have enabled Provincial to maintain a tramway system beyond the 1930s.

Bus operation in the Portsmouth area goes back a long way. There is evidence of a horse-bus on Portsea Island as long ago as 1840, while the first motor bus took to the streets in 1899, running along the sea-front between the piers during the summer. But before World War I the reliability of early motor vehicles left a lot to be desired, so that no serious competition to the trams came on the scene until 1919. As the cost of extending (or even updating) the tramway was sufficient to give anyone pause for thought, the infinitely cheaper and more flexible bus gained the chance to prove it could be a useful feeder to the trams, and possibly more. Southdown acquired a foothold with services into Portsmouth from Brighton, on what was later to become the immortal '31' (precursor of today's 700), but it is important to remember that one of Southdown's predecessors (and constituents in 1915) was the Sussex Road Car Company — which had been pioneering in Portsmouth back in 1907 with routes to Hambledon and Bognor! Some splendid anecdotes of those early days are recounted in *The Southdown Story 1915-1965*, copies of which are still obtainable from the Company. But it was in 1919 that Portsmouth Corporation first invested in the internal combustion machine, buying ten Thornycroft 'J' chassis and having them fitted with open-top double-deck bodies built by Wadhams at Waterlooville. The original bodies did not take kindly to the rough ride produced by a combination of solid tyres and cobbled streets; the view of Portsmouth Corporation's passengers in this matter has not been recorded. But while fitting all ten buses with similar second-hand open-top bodywork from redundant London General Omnibus Company 'B' types was considered justified from the mid-1920s onwards, the option to convert

*At the top of Portsdown Hill, outside The George Inn, Light Railway car no. 14 stands on single track in the middle of the road while a Foden steam lorry stops to 'blow up' after the climb from Purbrook. The photographer took advantage of the brief pause to take his picture over the shoulder of a motorman on another tram bound for Horndean, waiting for the single line section to be cleared before moving forward. (C.H.T. Marshall)*

*Greetham Street in 1930: the Royal Marines have marched from their barracks at Eastney to embark from the Town station (Portsmouth & Southsea), attracting the attention of old soldiers, friends and well-wishers on the way. In the background, one of the covered-top Corporation trams inches forward, while an assortment of wagons and carriages occupy the tracks alongside. Behind the hoardings on the left stands the goods depot, soon to be relocated at Fratton to make way for electrification of the lines to Brighton and Waterloo.*

the Thornycrofts to pneumatic tyres was not exercised. Apart from the handful of Guy 'Toastrack' single-deckers acquired in 1924 (nos. 11-15, TP 115-119) being converted in 1929, almost all future deliveries had pneumatic tyres as standard equipment — a statement that may cause readers accustomed to specifying low profile, tubeless radials for their cars, some amusement. The truth is the motor bus, let alone the private car, has come a long way in the past 70 years. The inter-war years saw a succession of Dennis and Thornycroft single-deckers join the Corporation fleet, with some huge three-axle Karrier vehicles to usher in the covered-top double-deck era. These bulky buses were not an outstanding success — and may even have prompted Portsmouth's early flirtation with the economies of diesel operation, whatever the price in dirty laundry caused by generous quantities of black exhaust fumes.

If the 1920s had been characterised mostly by single-deck vehicles, save where ample bridge clearances permitted the use of ungainly open-top or 'highbridge' covered-top double-deckers when these were manufactured towards the end of the decade, the 1930s marked the flowering of the motor bus everywhere. Standardisation made sense following the Depression, for it enabled economies of scale to streamline maintenance and cut costs. Portsmouth Corporation purchased substantial numbers of double-deckers with English Electric bodywork, with chassis manufactured by Leyland, Crossley and TSM (Tilling-Stevens); there was also a solitary AEC 'Regent' and the prototype Crossley 'Condor' as well as a handful of petrol-engined Leyland TD1s delivered with Short Brothers bodywork, plus two more bodied by Park Royal. Once the decision was made to abandon the tramways and replace them with trolleys, there was a further boost to the double-deck bus fleet. To begin with there was a pilot scheme of 15 trolleys, which were of

various different chassis types and combination of electrical equipment in order to find the most suitable for Portsmouth's requirements. After electing to proceed with the AEC 661T with English Electric equipment, the Corporation placed a vast order for the complete conversion programme. This amounted to a further 85 AEC trolley buses, nine bodied by English Electric and the remaining 76 by Cravens of Sheffield. New roads and housing developments both within the City and on its outskirts at Wymering, Farlington, Cosham and Hilsea called for enlargement of the motor bus numbers as well: 46 Leyland 'Titan' TD4 double-deckers with bodywork by English Electric (12), Leyland (4) and Cravens (30) supplemented 12 oil-engined TD2s that had come into service during 1933, to give the Corporation a modern fleet of vehicles with a high degree of standardisation and economy. The trolley buses began on 4 August 1934 and replaced the trams in stages within just over two years. In parts of the City it was possible to see all three forms of transport — trams, trolleys and motor buses - at work side by side during the interim period, but remarkably few photographs seem to exist showing this historic development. Mindful of the interest that transport arouses nowadays it is likely that if such scenes were possible at Cosham compound in 1990, for example, photographers would outnumber passengers.

The Corporation was not alone, of course, in embracing modernisation. Southdown rebodied many of its solid-tyred charabancs of the early 1920s, some with new open-top double-deck bus bodies by Shorts, and equipped the chassis with pneumatic tyres. The older Leyland 'N' and 'G7' chassis had only two-wheel brakes, but were deemed good enough to justify the money spent on conversion. However, once Leyland introduced the revolutionary 'Titan', the assortment of vehicles began to be

St. Mary's church tower provides the viewpoint for this unusual photograph, looking north along Kingston Road towards North End. Fratton Road had been improved and widened in 1928/9, which explains the sign 'Road Narrows' just in front of the telephone kiosk. The Southdown bus heading for Southsea is a new Leyland Titan TD1 with Short Bros. body incorporating a sunroof — it was this type of vehicle that posed serious competition to the Horndean trams — so the date is likely to be 1931/2. (The News, Portsmouth)

In August 1919 Portsmouth Corporation had taken delivery of its first motor buses — ten Thornycroft 'J' models with double-deck bodies by Wadhams. Their arrival was celebrated with some panache, including a procession past the Town Hall! This record of the occasion shows half a dozen of the hissing, spluttering novelties (with police escort) parading through Guildhall Square: no. 6 (BK 2982) is leading with the customary party of VIPs, while in the background is the Town station (Portsmouth & Southsea), the Goods Depot and an open-top tramcar. (Portsmouth City Record Office)

*The three-axle Karrier buses with double-deck bodies by either Brush or English Electric were licensed to carry 60 seated passengers — quite a large number in 1927. This rear view of no. 42 (TP 4705) illustrates the smart paintwork and vast bulk of the Brush double-deck body, also the unusual upper deck window arrangement. The bus was disposed of in 1935, displaced by the simple and reliable Leyland Titan TD4 diesels. (Portsmouth City Record Office)*

*One of the utility Daimler CWA6 buses supplied to Portsmouth Corporation during the war. No. 173 (CTP 167) shows off the angular Duple bodywork when parked in one of the City's terraced side streets in the late-1940s. Even austerity bodywork looked presentable when painted in the fully-lined colour scheme. (A.B. Cross)*

rationalised: for year after year, Leyland products made their way south, 'Titan' double-deckers, 'Tiger' single-deckers and coaches, 'Cub' lightweight buses and coaches, 'Cheetah' coaches, 'Lioness' and 'Tigress' tourers, in an endless procession. The first real break in that pattern came when supplies were disrupted by World War II and Leylands were no longer available for civilian use; Southdown was allocated 100 utility Guy 'Arab' double-deckers, of which perhaps a quarter came to the Portsmouth area. Some were painted grey, some had slatted wooden seats, some had no upper-deck rear window and all were angular in design compared with the shapely pre-war styles so much a hallmark of this company. Whereas the Leylands — whether petrol or diesel — exuded a certain charm, the Guys

were coarse and noisy. But, despite that, their rugged Gardner diesel engines and whistling transmissions kept going and going — and going! So impressive was the reliability of the utility 'Arab' that Southdown bought some Mark III and IV versions after the war was over. A handful of the original examples lasted in service for 20 years, while others were rebuilt to open-top form to replace the 1929 Leylands on summertime sea front duties until they, in turn, were ousted by a new breed of 'convertible' PD3 in 1964.

Portsmouth Corporation suffered from air-raids in the early years of the war, losing a number of buses as a result of a direct hit on Eastney depot in 1941. Among the losses were two nearly-new Leyland 'Cheetah' single-

*Wartime Portsmouth (1): With Portsdown Hill like a skating rink because of ice and snow, the buses that were dispersed from the City at night found themselves trapped by the cold snap in the morning. In this 1941 winter scene, double-deckers of both Southdown and the Corporation were stuck near The George — two Craven-bodied TD4s of the latter being in company with a TD1 and TD3 of Southdown. The 1929-vintage TD1 has been fitted with a temporary canvas roof, while one Corporation bus was in anonymous grey paint. (The News, Portsmouth)*

*Wartime Portsmouth (2): The Southern Railway called up ten of Stroudley's 'D1' 0-4-2Ts for fire-fighting duties. No. 2260 was allocated to Fratton shed after being fitted with a Shand Mason pump capable of directing a ton of water per minute from four powerful jets. It was first employed in earnest on the night of 17/18 April, 1941, and withdrawn for scrap in July 1946. (The News, Portsmouth)*

deckers out of a batch of six purchased in 1939, while the assorted prototype trolleys —which had no auxiliary batteries fitted to enable them to creep along when the overhead power supply was disrupted — were withdrawn for the rest of the war and stored on open ground at Northern Parade. The War Ministry sent 10 petrol-engined Bedford 'OWB' saloons and nine utility Daimler double-deckers to help out; all 19 remained active until the 1960s, the single-deckers re-seated to make them more comfortable and the double-deck CWA6s rebodied by Crossley to make them less ugly. I spent my early childhood in Portsmouth during those war years and have good reason to remember the Daimlers, numbered 171-179. They ap-

*Wartime Portsmouth (3): Traffic-jam for the war effort? Only authorised personnel could have a petrol allowance during the war, so it can be assumed that every car in this picture was driven by someone on official business. It is believed the photograph was taken in Northern Road between Cosham and Hilsea — the congestion could have been caused by an unexploded bomb scare, as several fell in the creek near Portsbridge. Two Southdown buses, a Harrington-bodied single-decker of the 1400 series followed by a lowbridge Titan double-decker possibly on the 38 service from Droxford, are stuck in the midst of a wonderful selection of pre-war motor cars. (The News, Portsmouth)*

peared regularly on the Copnor Road routes (A and B), but one might also be found on the Wymering to Highbury Estate service through Cosham High Street (circular routes J and K). In original austerity guise they had the slatted seats, which were varnished wood. It did not take one long to grasp that the Daimlers could accelerate as quickly as a trolley bus, thanks to the pre-select gearbox and fluid flywheel transmission, so it was good policy to hang on very tight when the conductor rang the bell to start. If one did not, you could easily end up sitting on the floor! I quite missed the angular bodywork of the utility Duple design, but it has to be said they were vastly more comfortable after rebodying. In their later years they were associated with the 145 service to Portchester, Cornaway Lane — the furthest west scheduled Corporation vehicles normally went.

To give a detailed account of all the buses and coaches to be seen in Portsmouth would justify a complete volume in itself. But I hope it may prove practical to give a view that captures the essence of the late 1940s and early 1950s, both in words and pictures, to convey something of the excitement of that vital period. Old and new, classic, utility or modern, the whole range from 1929 to 1949 could be seen at work side by side: while one inevitably had favourites, all were interesting and full of character. Perhaps my idea of Heaven would be a day trip back to 1948/9. Just imagine Portsmouth in the early months of 1948: petrol-driven double-decker Leyland 'Titan' TD1s still performing daily on routes E and F (Alexandra Park to Eastney and vice versa) via Chichester Road and Copnor Bridge, while new 'Titan' PD1s were coming into service on routes M and N (Leigh Park to Dockyard and vice versa). The PD1 appeared in Portsmouth livery from November 1947 and by the end of that year there were two, nos. 199 and 200 (DTP 808/9). Although Southdown had been operating PD1 chassis since the summer of 1946, with bodywork first by Park Royal (almost utility style) and then the handsome all-Leyland metal-framed product the follow-

No less than three Corporation Leyland Titan PD1 double-deckers appear in this view of Commercial Road, Portsmouth, near the junction with Edinburgh Road. Although taken in the mid-1950s, all these Weymann-bodied PD1s were delivered in 1948: the type gave excellent service and one remained in use as the driver-training vehicle until 1972. (The News, Portsmouth)

last vehicles had utility bodies built by another concern, but which were being strengthened and improved by Reading's to prolong their useful life now that the war was over; FRU 7/9 belonged to Hants & Dorset! With youthful curiosity I peeped inside the cab doors of each bus in turn — no one seemed to notice me in the dim half-light of a winter afternoon — and then, greatly daring, I flicked on the ignition warning light on one of the Guys. The urge to press the starter button was resisted with some difficulty, which was just as well because who knows what might have happened next?

The impulse to start a bus myself was to be satisfied sooner than I imagined. Having been familiar with the Southdown garage at Hilsea almost from the time I could walk, my attention became centred upon the Corporation depots at North End and Eastney. The former had a large allocation of trolleys, many of which remained in the Stygian depths except during the rush-hour; even then, some seemed to be stored out of use, dusty and forlorn. If one was quiet, it was quite possible to examine the destination blinds from end to end without attracting attention (and likely opprobrium!); it most probably explains a lifelong interest in such features. But if North End allowed undisturbed contemplation of trolleys and route indicators, it was to Eastney that one needed to go to see the most ancient motor buses. From school in Grove Road South that meant catching a Corporation vehicle, either a motor bus in Elm Grove on route C to Eastney Road

ing season, the different livery of the Corporation models made them stand out. Besides, they had bodies built by Reading's, whose premises were only a few hundred yards away from Hilsea Bastion, just south of the Coach and Horses. After my first couple of rides on 199, I wandered along to Reading's bodyshop to see if there were any more nearing completion — and got a shock! Inside the workshop stood a number of double-decker buses under construction, including DTP 809 (no. 200) being painted for the Corporation, but it was the rest that surprised me: two Guy 'Arab' models for Provincial (nos. 8 and 9; GHO 595/6), complete with Red Indian's head on the radiator, plus two more Guys — not new — which were receiving attention up in a corner. These

*This was Southsea in the first summer of peace after World War II. Viewed from one of the seafront hotels, the Canoe Lake and promenade look much the same as now — but the buses... An AEC 661T trolley sets off for Cosham (Railway Station) on service 4A, looking rather the worse for wear in shabby pre-war paint plus grey roof; a repainted Leyland Titan TD4, also with Craven bodywork, follows close behind on route B destined for Cosham Red Lion, while an elderly Crossley Condor in grey livery remains by the kerb — perhaps on route H for Green Lane via Copnor? In the background a Southdown Leyland Tiger with Harrington coach-work draws away on an excursion. (The News, Portsmouth)*

followed by a short walk, or a trolley via Albert Road direct to the depot. In 1948 on the C that would have been one of the many Leyland 'Titan' TD4 models — very possibly a 'V-front' of the all-Leyland quartet numbered 127-130 (RV 6370-73) — or an AEC 661T trolleybus on service 4, 17 or 18. On arrival at Eastney it was possible to see quite a lot just by looking through the open doors facing on to the main road, but the garage was so long that it was impractical to make everything out. There

was another entrance: walking along Methuen Road past all the little terraced houses with no more than 14 feet frontage, there was another set of doors and a pair of wrought iron gates beyond that, both beckoning access to the rear of the depot.

Public Relations is not a phenomenon unique to the 1980s and 90s, for nearly every bus operator throughout the ages has tried to impress passengers and public with the latest

*BUT 9611T trolleybus no. 311 (ERV 936) with 52-seat Burlingham bodywork was passing Eastney depot on route 6 for Palmerston Road and the Dockyard on 2 December, 1962, beneath a mass of overhead wiring. 15 of these smart vehicles formed the final series of trolleys delivered to Portsmouth Corporation during 1950/1. Inside the depot can be seen one of the little Bedford OWB saloons with Duple utility body (165: CTP 86) and a Weymann-style PD1, while a brace of Leyland Tiger Cub single-deckers (also bodied by Weymann) stand outside on the roadway. The trolleys were withdrawn after 27 July, 1963.*

*One of the splendid all-Leyland Titan PD2 double-deckers operated by the Corporation for many years — no. 70 (GTP 987) — emerges from the gloomy interior of North End depot. By the time this picture came to be taken the overhead trolley wires had vanished and the 25 examples of this type were nearing the end of their days with CPPTD. Today, few would suspect there had been a combined tram, trolley and bus depot in Gladys Avenue — the origins of which went back to 1874! The building was closed in November 1981.*

models; it follows that the more decrepit vehicles tend to linger near the back. Standing by the doorway in Methuen Road, I could spy several old Crossley 'Condor' double-deckers, a TSM E60A6 and some elderly Leyland TD1 or TD2 examples. All had the quaint little display with route letter in a separate box above the final destination and practically every one had English Electric bodywork. The open yard, through the gates, revealed more of the mid-Thirties machinery and

*Memories of Portsmouth (1): Lower Church Path was a pedestrian-only walkway situated between Arundel Street and Surrey Street, fronting into the busy Commercial Road. Here a driver and his daughter return from buying an ice cream, while in the background Edinburgh Road looks quiet. Notice the Triumph coach with Harrington 'dorsal fin' bodywork in the middle of the road and Finlays shop by the level crossing: the date is around 1950. (The News, Portsmouth)*

9414), the last new double-deck motor bus to be delivered to Portsmouth before the war. "Hop up in there, lad" he said, so I scrambled with some difficulty into the high cab of the Craven-bodied vehicle. The steps seemed so far off the ground, and the grab-handles must have been designed for giants, but at last I was perched on the leather seat with my feet on the pedals. "Do you want to start it up for me?" "Yes, please", I whispered, almost too excited for words. He told me what to do: switch on the ignition on the fascia panel, make sure the gearstick was in neutral, press down the accelerator pedal and push the starter. The engine began to spin over, quite slowly at first for it was 'cold', then one by one the cylinders began to 'fire' before the 8.6 litre unit came to life. "Keep your foot down" I was told, while acrid fumes swirled all around, so I sat there keeping the engine running at fast tickover speed for a couple of minutes, until it was warm enough to leave to its own devices. Small wonder, perhaps, that CPPTD no. 160 ever thereafter had a special place among my transport interests, though it seems to have been inclined to be camera-shy.

Leaving Eastney for home, one or two more examples of the new post-war 'Titan' (the PD1) were in evidence on Copnor Road routes A and B. Numbered between 180 and 198, they formed a series from a different coachbuilder — Weymann —providing fresh interest when comparing them with the Reading-built buses.

a wartime Bedford as well as a 'Cheetah' — that model's Wadham bodywork was blessed with no less than eight destination blinds. Before leaving I went to have one last look through the doorway at the vintage collection within, and was promptly spotted by a Corporation employee. To my relief I was not bawled out, in fact he asked what I was interested in. He called me over and took me all along the line of silent vehicles, while I feverishly scribbled their numbers on a page in my school exercise book. That page has long since been lost, but the impressions of that visit are still sharp. Finally, he asked if I had ever sat in the cab: I shook my head, which was true as far as Corporation buses went. He pointed across to a Leyland 'Titan' TD4 — it was no. 160 (RV

*Memories of Portsmouth (2): The floating bridge between Point, Old Portsmouth and Gosport was provided by a pair of ancient steam-driven vessels Alexandra and Duke of York, working alternatively. A post-war Wolseley car disembarks on the Gosport side while one of the passenger launches approaches the pontoon with a full complement. On the far side of the Harbour are the tall chimneys of the power station, some of the well-known public houses of Old Portsmouth, the Cathedral and the Round Tower. (The News, Portsmouth)*

With their metal-framed bodies, the Corporation was to obtain excellent value from its first generation of post-war buses; one survived on driver training duties until 1972. But whatever the good qualities of the 7.4 litre-engined PD1s, they were eclipsed by the PD2. Southdown's first supplies, again with the Leyland metal-framed body, started to appear in the spring of 1948 and before long Hilsea had a substantial allocation. With beefy 9.8 litre engines under the bonnet, some equipped with synchromesh gears, the PD2's performance was almost on a par with the thirsty petrol-engined 'Titan' TD1 but with consumption around 10 mpg on diesel fuel. Seating 56, the 80 examples of the PD2/1 that Southdown bought in 1948 were trend-setters all along the South Coast. Where a pre-war diesel, or even the post-war PD1, would labour up Portsdown Hill in the rush-hour with a standing load, the

*Memories of Portsmouth (3): From the footbridge in Greetham Street, a view of Portsmouth & Southsea station in about 1930. In the foreground are dozens of wagons in the former goods depot before it was transferred to Fratton: all the old post-Grouping companies — GWR, LMS, LNER (NE) and Southern — are represented in this pre-electrification picture, with an Iron Mink van nearest the camera. The row of intricate posts supporting the overhead tram wires leads down to the Guildhall, while a freight train labours up the ramp to the High Level platforms on its way to the Dockyard. (The News, Portsmouth)*

PD2 would walk away and, once over the brow, swoop along in a most exhilarating fashion. Although some did share duties with older buses on Havant Road services, including the 31 through to Brighton, Hilsea put them to work mostly on routes over Portsdown Hill, where their superior power and speed showed up to instant advantage. It was another four years before the Corporation caught on, but thereafter as the trolley bus went out of favour so more PD2s (and even five of the 30 feet long PD3s) came to take their place. Southdown, in the meantime, ordered the 8 feet wide model (the '700 series') which spread everywhere except westwards to Fareham — at least, not for some years.

Southdown was not completely in

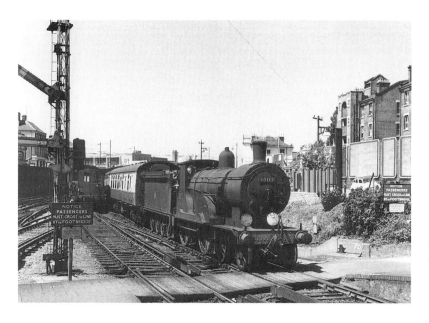

Memories of Portsmouth (4): Standing on Fratton station beneath the footbridge over which generations of Pompey supporters must have tramped, no one could forget the sound of a Drummond 4-4-0 passing through on song. Class T9 Greyhound no. 30117 makes music as it accelerates the 12.15 pm Portsmouth & Southsea to Plymouth train through non-stop on 8 July, 1959, the staccato beat drowning out the exhaust of Hampshire diesel set 1106 heading in the opposite direction. Fratton bridge is in the background, complete with trolley wires.

Memories of Portsmouth (5): Fratton MPD and locomotive roundhouse. Standard class 4MT 2-6-0 no. 76068 simmered quietly outside the shed in the final week of October, 1963, with the breakdown train at the back of the siding. Under British Railways the shed was first coded 71D, becoming 70F after reorganisation in the 1950s; by this date it was no more than a signing-on point for crews and had no official allocation at all. The building was demolished in the early Seventies.

Leyland's pocket. During 1948/9 the 12 Guy 'Arab' Mark III models with Northern Counties bodywork came on stream. Though lacking the top speed of the Leylands, their ability to slog up Portsdown Hill was equal to the PD2s and noticeably more lively than the PD1s. They worked the shorter routes to Purbrook, Stakes, Waterlooville, Denmead and Hambledon particularly, when new, before largely monopolising the 38 to Droxford and beyond once the Corporation's PD2s (numbered 58-82; GTP 975-999) took over the 37 and 37A duties from 1953. A development took place on the Hayling road, too: the growing traffic to and from Havant and the surrounding area could scarcely be contained with an ageing fleet of pre-war single-deckers, so 10 new Dennis 'Falcon' saloons were required for the 1949 season. Fitted with 30-seater bodies by the chassis manufacturer, numbers 82 to 91 (JUF 82-91) were to be a stop-gap measure until the new bridge was constructed at Langstone. Along with two Bedford 'OB' coaches with Duple 'Vista' bodies, suitable for excursion work and relief express duties when required, these vehicles were the last to be ordered for Southdown specifying petrol engines.

There was one significant change for Southdown that was to leave its mark on double-deck design for a generation. Not content with ordering 30 ft. long buses, Southdown standardised on full-fronted Northern Counties bodywork for its 285 Leyland 'Titan' PD3s delivered between 1957 and 1967. Thirty 'convertible' versions built in 1964/5 lasted well into the 1980s, and one or two, retained for special duties, have been restored to traditional Southdown livery for the Nineties.

In retrospect, perhaps the saddest decision made by Portsmouth Corporation in the 1950s was to abandon the trolley buses. There was much public debate and heated argument, a report by experts to support the Council's view and a gradual run-down of the system, which closed completely on 27 July 1963. Only 15 post-war trolleys were built, BUT 9611T models with unusual 52-seat Burlingham bodywork, delivered in 1950/1. In their place came the Corporation's first Leyland 'Atlantean' rear-engined double-deckers, numbered 201 to 225 (201-225 BBK), which were quickly followed by a further 10 vehicles (226-235 CRV) all with 76-seat bodies by Metro-Cammell Weymann. Though I have never been enthusiastic about rear-engined buses, it has to be said that Portsmouth's early 'Atlanteans' were among the most attractive of their kind; the time-honoured livery suited them well. While certain quirks manifested themselves with these new vehicles and heavy-docking intervals came down from around 250,000 miles to below 100,000 initially, their increased seating capacity helped at peak periods and enabled some rationalisation of routes to take place, especially to the large estates of Paulsgrove and Leigh Park. The pity was in the wastage of an entire system, the growing menace of both noise and pollution coupled with the failure to heed the lessons of the Suez Crisis (1956). With the benefit of hindsight, thirty years on, shouldn't the trolleys have been extended at least to Paulsgrove and Farlington, if not right through to Havant?

Though it may seem incredible, the veteran quartet of open-top TD4s were still hard at work each summer until September 1971 on the Sea Front service 25 in Portsmouth. Kitted out with more modern headlamps and a reversed livery, 1935-built Titan no. 6 (RV 6360; formerly no. 117) had a good load on from Hayling Ferry when it approached South Parade Pier on 25 May, 1969. More modern coaches wait for custom alongside the promenade, including Byngs, White Heather and Southdown.

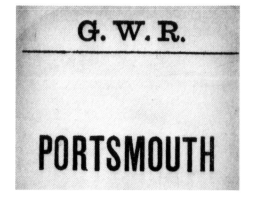

# 8 · FULL CIRCLE?
## *All Change!*

The conclusion of the 1960s marked a sort of watershed in transport development. Cessation of production of traditional front-engined designs of double-deck buses, the Beeching period of retrenchment and abandonment of steam traction on British Railways, the last coal-fired paddle steamer operating across the Solent: all these events heralded the end of a well-established order. The origin of the last new Leyland 'Titan' PD3 delivered to Southdown in 1967 could be traced back to the company's first 'Titan' TD1 of 1929 — one of which still remained in its ownership after retirement from tree-lopping duties — while the Southern Region of British Rail finished scrapping steam locomotives on the Isle of Wight in 1967 that William Adams had designed for LSWR suburban trains in 1889. The trolley bus, logical successor of the electric tramcar, was being discarded not only along the South Coast at Brighton, Portsmouth, Reading and, finally, Bournemouth but also throughout the country. As the decade drew to a close, it felt like turning an important page of history.

British Railways has shrunk considerably in track mileage since Nationalisation in 1948, but it was only with the passing of the steam locomotive in the South after 9 July, 1967, that the symbolic affinity with the Industrial Revolution was lost. In all the preceding chapters we have looked at transport, road and rail as well as a glimpse of the coastal shipping where appropriate, in a historical context; in this one all the strands of the narrative are brought together for the Seventies and Eighties. As the Sixties slipped away it was as though the stately progression of change that had been the hallmark of transport development up to that time was being thrown over-board. Man had landed on the moon in 1969, and all our horizons were enlarged in consequence. Television, spacecraft and computers fired the imagination of the up and coming generations, making steam trains, paddle steamers and front-engined buses seem extraordinarily dated. It was as if mankind was turning its back on all the achievements of the past in order to grasp the superficial attractions of nuclear power and the microchip. No society could withstand such momentous changes, so quickly, without some ripples; those who have lived through the 1970s and 1980s may be inclined to think those ripples had more in common with hurricane-force winds or towering waves!

One factor that was to have a major influence on the course of events through-out those two decades was inflation. It was not new, of course, but the rate at which the value of money was being eroded by the rising cost of living had never been so high within living memory. The upward pressure was given a boost by the change to decimal currency in 1971, itself a prelude to Britain becoming a member of the European Community. Whilst I am in no way denigrating the fact that Britain joined the EC in 1973, the results have

For all their standardisation, not all Nationals were the same: at the new Hard Interchange, built out over the mudflats of Portsmouth Harbour, Southdown no. 88 (YCD 88T) was leaving on a Limited Stop service 702 for Hayling Island while CPPTD no. 102 (KCR 102P) remained ticking-over before departure to Aylen Road (Green Lane) on route 11. The green bus was 11.3m long while the white/crimson vehicle had the shorter specification of 10.3m with twin doors. The Interchange alongside Portsmouth Harbour station was opened on 18 May, 1979 ; the Portsmouth National was withdrawn on 31 October, 1981, after little more than five years' life!

One of the few rural bus services to survive — and then only thanks to support from Hampshire County Council — is the 38 between Portsmouth and Droxford. On 4 May, 1985, CPPTD sent one of its three Dennis Lancet midibuses over the hill to Southwick, Wickham and Droxford on one of the infrequent journeys to the Meon Valley — no. 95 (GTP 95X) was the only example of the Wadham-Stringer Vanguard bodies to have coach seats. The little vehicle has turned off the main A32 just north of The Roebuck to climb up through the lovely Forest of Bere at Mislingford between Wickham and Soberton.

*Provincial in the early days under NBC control: Hoeford depot in 1971 could still offer a fascinating selection of buses ranging from double-deckers of the Forties to hybrid Guy-Deutz creations unique to this fleet. This cameo outside the venerable tramway shed shows the sole single-deck Guy-Deutz no. 37 (HOR 676E; formerly no. 8), second-hand Guy Arab III no. 25 (FCR 445; formerly no. 40) which came from Southampton Corporation and AEC Regent no. 66 (975 CWL) that originated with City of Oxford — all are painted in the brighter Emerald and County Cream livery introduced in the late-1960s.*

*The minibus era came upon Provincial in the form of the Iveco Daily with Robin Hood body, during the latter part of 1986. Though still painted in NBC green and white, the old company's garter was featured on the sloping front, surrounding traditional style fleet numbers. On 21 November, 1986, no. 117 (D117 DRV) negotiates the narrow bridge at Knowle when returning from Hedge End to Fareham on route 75 — until their arrival, no scheduled bus service operated between Wickham and Knowle via Mayles Lane. Only one journey in each direction on the 75 ran via Knowle.*

*Full circle, indeed! Fareham provides the backcloth to a quiet revolution in taste on the buses: on the left one of Provincial's indigenous Leyland National single-deckers (17: HOR 417L) from the 1972 intake, still wears the drab NBC uniform — while a recent recruit from South Wales looks immaculate in a livery that began with the company's tramcars around the turn of the century (no. 86; NWO 490R). The location is West Street, where the former Wesleyian chapel stood opposite the cinema; the year is 1989.*

been far-reaching and continue to have an effect on our daily lives — an ongoing process for which no end is yet in sight. European laws and regulations, particularly in the field of transport, are an established part of the way things are today: this trend is likely to accelerate during the 1990s with the need to adopt 'green', environment-friendly policies on exhaust emissions, global warming, acid rain and other issues that are beginning to have world-wide significance. Inflation has hastened the speed with which things happen. For example, in 1968 the National Bus Company was just being formed as a result of the merger of the former Tilling Group's interests (which had been nationalised) with the bus companies previously owned by the BET Group (in the private sector). This vast conglomerate created by an ill-starred marriage was not likely to be an easy thing to control, even in a stable financial climate; in the bumpy monetary conditions Britain experienced during the 1970s — inflation at 25% per annum and more, strictures imposed by the IMF, damaging strikes — the National Bus Company was doomed to have a short life-expectancy. Old rivals, such as Hants & Dorset, Southdown, Provincial and Aldershot & District (Alder Valley), suddenly became uneasy bedfellows while others — like Chisnell's King Alfred buses in Winchester —were swallowed wholesale and disappeared without trace. Except where bus services were maintained by town and city councils, for example in Portsmouth, Southampton and Bournemouth, the NBC flying N symbol became the norm. Traditional liveries were displaced by National Green or National Red, sometimes with white relief, so that it was no longer possible to recognise instantly to which fleet a bus belonged.

This state of affairs was not made easier by the increasing use of all-over advertising on buses, plus the practice of switching vehicles from one NBC subsidiary to another. Further

blurring of individual identities came about through ever-increasing standardisation of design: a Leyland National from Alder Valley was not noticeably different from a Leyland National licensed by Hants & Dorset, both of which might be seen in Poppy Road paintwork in Petersfield or Winchester. As older types of vehicle were withdrawn, the less variety remained. The standard NBC colour schemes and fleet-name style became mandatory from 1972, together with the N symbol; whilst some small degree of variation in their application occurred with the passage of time, this was officially discouraged.

Some changes to local authority boundaries and titles came in 1974: Portsmouth Corporation became Portsmouth City Council, Alton and Petersfield combined to form East Hampshire District Council and so on. By the mid-1980s this led to the formation of independent bus companies such as Portsmouth City Transport Limited, Southampton City Bus and Yellow Buses (in place of Bournemouth Corporation), thereby distancing the municipalities from direct involvement by the time of de-regulation in October 1986. These changes took place against the background of contrasting political attitudes, the gradual process of centralisation set in train in 1945 being abruptly reversed after 1979. Ratepayers have been relieved of the day-to-day operation of bus services, although Hampshire County Council and its neighbours support a number of socially necessary but unremunerative routes to ensure a basic network beyond that likely to be provided on a purely commercial foundation. These 'contracted' services have their counterparts in those railway routes subsidised by central government as being socially necessary but unlikely to be self-supporting under approved financial criteria. Let us take a closer look at some particular instances that have happened in the past 20 years.

*Meeting of the clans at Midhurst in the 1980s. Two independents mingle with two NBC subsidiaries, representing (left to right) Southern Motorways (B.S. Williams Ltd), Alder Valley, Arrow Travel and Southdown. The Plaxton-bodied Ford R1114 was working the old Hants & Sussex route to Stedham (service 26) acquired from W.A. Potter in 1947; Alder Valley's National prepared to operate the Aldershot & District service 19 (now 219) back to Aldershot; a Willowbrook-bodied Daimler Roadliner new in 1971 showed Pulborough on the blind while Southdown's fame rested on an ECW-bodied Bristol VRT double-decker.*

*Southampton Citybus (formerly City of Southampton Transport) has begun investing in a new generation of single-deck buses. As the National was never operated, the choice of Leyland Lynx was unexpected but no. 103 (F103 RTR) found employment on the former Hants & Dorset route 50 between Petersfield and Southampton in 1989. Still in a sort of off-white undercoat when pictured in Droxford in the early part of the year, no. 103 has since been painted in full Southampton red and cream livery.*

One bus route that has fascinated me for as long as I can ever remember is the 38 from Portsmouth to Droxford. Started by Blue Motor Services of Boarhunt, it was taken over by Southdown from 16 September, 1935, running between Clarence Pier and Hambledon via Portsdown Hill, Southwick, Wickham, Soberton, Droxford and Meonstoke. During the war services ran from Portsmouth (Thea-

tre Royal) to Droxford only, being allowed 1 hour 26 minutes during the 'black out'. When peacetime operations could be resumed on 13 May, 1945, it was extended again to Meonstoke and an additional 38A service introduced to serve Newtown. For the summer season in 1951, 38 started from the Floating Bridge in Old Portsmouth, but this was not repeated in subsequent years; instead it reverted to the pre-war terminus at Clarence Pier between May and September from 1952-1958. A major extension to the northern end of the route came about on 6 February, 1955, following the closure of the Meon Valley railway line: for the first time Southdown double-deck buses continued beyond Meonstoke through West Meon, Privett, East Tisted and Farringdon to Alton Railway Station. The pattern did not alter much until Sunday services were withdrawn in 1971. Then, with one-man operated vehicles — usually single-deckers — being used, the only other economy open to Southdown was to cut back to Droxford. This sad but unavoidable step was taken in January 1974: the stage carriage licence together with a solitary Bristol 'RESL' bus was transferred to Alder Valley for the Alton to Droxford section, which was renumbered 59 and operated twice daily on weekdays only for schoolchildren, primarily. It connected at Droxford with the truncated Southdown service, itself renumbered 350, until the 59 from Alton became a casualty of Alder Valley retrenchment later in the decade. For a while a shoppers' service (205) ran infrequently through the Meon Valley corridor to Portsmouth, but it was so seldom I never saw it! The Southdown 350 route, with 450 short working to and from HMS Dryad at Southwick, survived on weekdays until the 1980s. Then, rather surprisingly, Southdown handed over just the 350 service to the CPPTD who promptly renumbered it 38.

Though loadings were generally light, as might be expected of a largely rural route, Eastney depot did not have many single-deckers to hand. If none of the seven Series 2 Leyland Nationals or three Dennis 'Lancet' midibuses was available, a double-deck Leyland 'Atlantean' might be substituted at short notice. Southdown had formerly kept the trees lopped to clear double-deckers, but when that practice fell into disuse, increasing damage to

front domes and even upper-deck windows prompted the route's designation as a single-deck duty; after all, Southdown had plenty of Leyland Nationals. But Portsmouth had sold off its 14 P-registered Mark 1s when they were scarcely five years old (nos. 101-114; KCR 101P etc.), at the same time as the historic North End depot was closed in November 1981. The rare single-deck 'Atlantean' model, introduced in 1971, had been reduced from 12 to just a couple for the Continental Ferry Port service, towing a luggage trailer, so it was hardly an option. The dilemma was not resolved until the kaleidoscope — after being well and truly shaken, following an uneasy transition from municipal to private-sector ownership with the title of Portsmouth City Bus — settled again. De-regulation has produced some odd results, but the sight of a Red Admiral Iveco minibus on the 38 at Droxford Square in April 1989 was not the most obvious scenario. Acquisition of some ex-London Leyland Nationals, similar to those bought new by Portsmouth in 1976 but then sold off in 1981, has alleviated the difficulty. As for liveries, the traditional colours of Crimson and White, introduced soon after Portsmouth was raised to the status of a city in the late-1920s, lingered until privatisation though with a greater preponderance of the latter. This White was the same shade as that used by NBC fleets, and became increasingly bleak when scoured by an automatic bus-washing plant; the limited areas of Crimson soon looked dull without the benefit of hand-washing. The revised livery introduced following the metamorphosis into Portsmouth City Bus was very similar to Southampton City Bus, which owned a substantial stake in the company after an earlier deal with Isle of Wight-based Southern Vectis fell through, Many of the vehicles were repainted in the City Bus style, vastly improving the overall impression. In the autumn of 1989 it was all change once more when Portsmouth joined Southdown and Hampshire Bus (amongst others) in the Stagecoach empire. A move later examined by the Monopolies and Mergers Commission and Secretary of State for Trade, Nicholas Ridley, who suggested in July, 1990, that they divest themselves of it as soon as practicable, whereupon Devon General came on to the scene — and so it goes on.

Provincial, once the holding company of a number of thriving tramway concerns in various parts of the country, had but a single remaining subsidiary after 1936. This was the Gosport & Fareham Omnibus Company (until 1929 named the Portsmouth Street Tramways Company) centred on Hoeford. In 1940 H. Orme White, who had been based at Grimsby until that tramway system closed down, became Manager and Engineer: for more than a quarter of a century he held sway at Hoeford, and his enterprise and flair for innovation is still remembered. It is inconceivable the company would not have remained independent if he had still been there in 1970, but he finally retired (aged 80-plus) in 1967 when his last two Guy-Deutz air-cooled buses were licensed. So Provincial was sold to the NBC, and from 31 December 1969 the holding company ceased to exist. But the statutory Gosport and Fareham Omnibus Company continued under the wing of the nationalised Hants & Dorset fleet, whose Head Office was in Bournemouth. In time the cramped Hants & Dorset servicing facilities at the Bus Station in West Street, Fareham — little changed since the place was built in 1931 — were closed and the staff merged with those from Provincial at Hoeford. Both fleets remained technically separate, with Hants & Dorset vehicles painted in Poppy Red and those of Gosport & Fareham (which retained the Provincial fleetname) in Leaf Green. By around 1980 the vast Hants & Dorset amalgam was trying to win new customers by focusing on the local image: of the seven names

dreamed up as a result of the MAP (Market Analysis Project) surveys in the late-1970s, Provincial was pulled out of the hat for — surprise, surprise! — the Gosport and Fareham area. This local exercise did not last very long, partly because the vinyl stickers soon peeled off after a few circuits of the bus-wash but also because the Hants & Dorset empire was to be carved up. After 31 March 1983 all routes east of Southampton, whether Hants & Dorset or Provincial, became the birth-right of the 'new' Provincial; north of Southampton was Hampshire Bus and west was the revived Wilts & Dorset. The next step was the disposal on the open market of all the NBC subsidiary companies.

Some, like Southdown and Wilts & Dorset, became management buy-outs. However, Provincial under the leadership of the energetic and resourceful James Freeman, became an employee-owned company (ESOP) with the majority of its 300 staff holding shares. This gave everyone a sense of pride and responsibility, the title People's Provincial Buses becoming the new trading name. After more than a decade as a single-deck only fleet of buses, a handful of double-deckers obtained second-hand now complement the serried ranks of Leyland Nationals and Iveco mini-buses, for school contracts or summer seasonal duties. The NBC green has given way to the former Emerald and Cream, with Brunswick Green for the lower skirt (in place of the old-style wings) and red wheels. A charming touch is provided by the traditional Provincial 'garter' or belt, surrounding the fleet number — a feature dating back to the tramway period. If Leyland National buses had been delivered new to Provincial in such a fine livery in 1972, they would have had instant appeal; as it is, their smart paintwork now is immediately recognisable from Park Gate to Portsmouth, from Stokes Bay to Southampton. I am sure

*Scarcely a ripple disturbs the Hamble river at Bursledon as Brush A1A-A1A no. 31.294 throttles back crossing the bridge with the 12.56 pm from Portsmouth Harbour to Bristol (Temple Meads) on 23 October, 1978. Since the end of steam there have been diesel multiple units and loco-hauled carriages on these cross-country services with varying degrees of success, but now the Sprinter era (and electrification) has changed the pattern.*

Grandfather would have been pleased to know his dream of Provincial linking Gosport with Portsmouth has been fulfilled at last.

There are other landmarks to note. Basil Williams' Hants & Sussex fleet, which began in April, 1937, has charted a complicated route through the passing years and absorbed a number of small country bus operators in the process. Although the vehicles carried the Southern Motorways name from the mid-1950s until 1987, the original title was revived for the founder's Golden Jubilee. Now ex-London AEC 'Swift' single-deckers can be seen in East Hampshire and West Sussex in colours reminiscent of those used from the 1940s to the

*Transport Milestones (1): Last of the front-engined double-deckers supplied to Southdown were the Northern Counties-bodied Leyland Titan PD3/4s of 1967. No. 367 (HCD 367E) in full NBC livery motors down Portland Street in Fareham towards the Quay Street roundabout — service 452 was a Monday-Friday only duty via the A.S.W.E. base on Portsdown Hill on route to Southsea (The Circle), probably the only one to terminate there in recent years. The Toby Jug and adjoining buildings were demolished during the 1980s. Progress?*

*Transport Milestones (2): A summer seasonal tour of Portsmouth was begun during the late-1970s. Numbered 101, this service commenced at the Canoe Lake, close to South Parade Pier, and featured a commentary by qualified guides for the benefit of tourists. One Sunday in 1984 two Leyland Atlantean AN68s were laying-over between trips at East Street, Old Portsmouth — East Lancs-bodied no. 346 (CPO 346W) contrasted with Alexander-bodied no. 311 (HOR 311N) not far from where Provincial once stabled horses for its trams.*

late-1960s, operating routes once the preserve of Bedford 'OB' or ex-LTE Guy GS 'Special' single-deckers. Southern Vectis extricated itself from the National Bus Company in the mid-Eighties and continues to dominate public transport in the Isle of Wight. In a bold move to break out of its Island straight-jacket, it promoted a new company on the mainland called Solent Blue Line with a distinctive livery — yellow and two shades of blue. It provides local services around Southampton, Eastleigh, Romsey and on the western shore of Southampton Water; many of these routes were taken over from Hampshire Bus, formed from part of Hants & Dorset in 1983.

The northern part of Hampshire Bus, mainly centred on Basingstoke, was bought by the Scottish-based Stagecoach Group following privatisation. It has an eye-catching 'house' livery of multi-coloured stripes on a plain white back-ground which, once seen, is not likely to be mistaken in the future. This livery has been progressively applied to all Group vehicles upon repaint: with the acquisition of both Southdown and Portsmouth City Bus during 1989, it was already extending eastwards along the South Coast. In the interim, one has sometimes found an erstwhile Portsmouth 'Atlantean' on the 42 service at Petersfield — a route that Southdown oper-

*Inside the new Maintenance Depot at Bournemouth, between Branksome and the former terminus at West station, showing new 442 Wessex Electric unit 2403 over the inspection pit. Normal service with these stylish 100 mph five-car sets commenced between Waterloo and Weymouth on 16 May, 1988.*

ated with that number until NBC policy caused it to be changed to 749 in 1982. Plus ça change, plus la même chose!

And what of British Railways during these past 20 turbulent years? Having cast aside the messy, inefficient steam locomotive it was necessary to establish in the public mind an alternative image. The management of BR set about achieving this in a number of ways: first, the very title was officially shortened to 'British Rail' for everyday usage, then an entirely different corporate colour scheme for trains was brought into use. The XP64 experi-

ment was a harbinger of things to come, for main line trains were painted in the blue and grey livery with which we have all been familiar for the past two decades and more; at first suburban multiple units, whether diesel or electric, were all blue but this gradually gave way during the 1980s to the blue and grey. One of the most significant developments within the area described in this book has been the 'new look', of Network South-East. After years of apparent stalemate on the railway, following the impact of the HST-125 diesel train, the marketing of the south-east corner of England as a comprehensive 'entity' in its own right is

Coming events casting their shadows before? The Delme viaduct at Fareham throbs with the all-out effort of a 73 electro-diesel locomotive hauling three multiple-unit electric sets eastwards towards Cosham, Havant and Brighton. This ECS train required diesel power because the tracks were not then electrified but, since May 1990, similar 4-VEP (423) units work under their own power from the electric third-rail now installed.

Basic railway: In bright new Network South-East livery, 4-CIG (421) unit no. 1253 stands by the buffer-stops at Lymington Pier, terminus of the five-mile branch from Brockenhurst, while the Sealink car ferry Cenwulf is berthed alongside. No frills and bus-stop type shelters characterise the NSE approach to many unstaffed stations like this, but bus and ship connections could hardly be simpler

When the railway came to Fareham and Gosport in 1841 the height of road traffic was not an issue — so long as there was a bridge of adequate height, the railway had fulfilled its statutory obligation! Newgate Lane bridge has barely 10 feet clearance, so a new elevated roadway was built to obviate the need for a higher bridge beneath the railway. 21 November, 1986, was the first day on which road and rail used the new ungated level crossing south of Fareham, when Crompton 33.114 returned from the stump of the original Gosport route with a short freight from Bedenham towards the junction.

quite novel. On 21 June, 1986, upon payment of a ridiculously small charge, it was possible to explore the entire area of Network South-East — including the London Underground — for the day: bounded by Weymouth, Whimple, Bedwyn, Banbury, Northampton, Bedford, Huntingdon, Cambridge, Harwich and everywhere to the south and east of London, it was an incredible bargain and publicity coup. Thousands of additional people travelled on the railway and many extra trains were laid on compared with a normal Saturday; the only services not included were those provided by HSTs and boat trains. For the first time it was possible to explore routes of the erstwhile 'Big Four' plus the tubes on just one ticket. At Waterloo and Marylebone, Paddington and Liverpool Street one could see initial examples of old and commonplace trains painted in the bright new NSE livery, while here and there a start had been made on tidying up stations with revised signs and fresh colours. It was bold and rather brash, but it gave the 'ordinary' railway (as opposed to the Inter-City flagship) a leg up into the latter half of the 20th century. Where Jimmy Savile and the Awayday syndrome had left off, Network South-East made the familiar seem new.

There must have been times recently when, far away from the confessional and the media, some people in BR wished they could undo the Beeching years and their aftermath. Senseless closures, like the Swanage branch and the Mid-Hants route from Alton to Winchester, look pretty silly when one sees the long tail-backs on our main roads. In the changed climate of investment in the railways, it is easy to imagine how useful both lines would be if they were still part of BR today. Electrification would certainly have been an option, just as it has been from Bournemouth to Weymouth. The stylish 100 mph 'Wessex Electric' class 442 units are, with some justifi-

cation, the showpiece of third-rail electrification since their introduction in May 1988. Now the forgotten tracks between Farlington, Portcreek Junction, Fareham and Eastleigh or St. Denys are being equipped with a third-rail with the current being switched on for testing from 12 March, 1990. Costing £17 million, the Solent Link scheme opens up all sorts of interesting possibilities for the future, as well as allowing replacement of the noisy and increasingly decrepit Hampshire diesel sets on local services. One can envisage possible revival of a Brighton — Bournemouth (and Weymouth?) train, while there are definite plans to have regular services between Southampton and Gatwick Airport. As a regular commuter myself, I look forward to direct travel from Fareham to Waterloo (and back!), something that has not been possible without changing at either Eastleigh or Fratton/Portsmouth since the days of steam from London to Gosport.

Diesel trains will still appear at Portsmouth (and Brighton) as part of the Regional Railways' cross-country services based on Cardiff. Loco-hauled rakes of four or five ageing Mark I carriages were replaced in 1988 by twin-car class 155 'Sprinter' units. When these were withdrawn temporarily for modification some 'Super Sprinter' class 156 sets were drafted in, but operation has now reverted to the earlier Leyland-built type. There are plans for the 155 units to be converted to single-cars (class 153) for more rural duties elsewhere, but the timing will depend on when the 'Express Sprinter' class 158 sets come on stream to replace them. Certainly, with 90 mph capability and air-conditioning, the mid-1990s look promising for cross-country travellers using the class 158 trains. The only caveat is that, if the stylish 158s generate as much business as their 'Wessex Electric' counter-parts, the two-coach sets may not be enough to cope with increased loads for very long. When the origi-

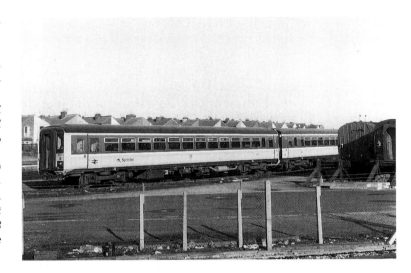

*New-look cross-country train: Sprinter diesel-electric units were introduced on Portsmouth to Bristol and Cardiff services with the commencement of the summer timetable in 1988. Before then, crew training and familiarisation were needed and one two-coach, 155 was sent to Fratton for that purpose. Leyland-built set 311 (155.311) was berthed on a siding parallel with Goldsmith Avenue in Portsmouth when not on test runs; during 1991 class 158 Express Sprinter units will take over the route.*

nal Hampshire diesels were introduced in 1957, it was soon found that an intermediate (third) carriage was essential. We shall have to wait and see.

What of the future? After 150 years of railways from London to the major destinations around the Solent, how are things likely to shape up in the years ahead? Gazing into a crystal ball, I would suggest that increasing saturation on all main roads and motorways can only point one way: a revival of rail-based transport, whether main line or urban LRT (Light Rapid Transit). The electric car, even if and when it becomes a commercial proposition, can by its nature cater for only a handful of passengers in each vehicle. A single-deck bus or coach can carry 50, a double-decker maybe 80 or more. Articulated tramcars of the latest European pattern can move around double that number on designated tracks — and without pollution. A twin-car 'Sprinter' is capable of shifting 200 over quite long distances, while even the existing electric multi-

ple unit sets of four or five coaches carry 300-plus passengers, with the facility to tack another set on to the same train and double the numbers. The flexibility, speed and greater safety of rail-based transport is beginning to win friends where, a quarter of a century ago, it seemed practically doomed to a slow demise. Add to that advantages based on environmental considerations and one has a powerful argument in its favour. Because it is simply not practical to serve every household by rail on a door-to-door basis, there will always be a need for road transport to act as a feeder, but I submit the proper balance should be tilted towards rail. It is truly amazing that new business parks have been constructed without rail access — the scope for a substantial shift of freight traffic of all kinds from road to rail is enormous and if implemented, would have a major impact on improving the quality of life. Britain has a long way to go before the disastrous legacy of the Sixties has been eradicated — neglected buildings, abandoned trackbeds, lost traffic — but the tide has turned.

Since the demise of Hants & Dorset on 31 March, 1983, and its split into four smaller companies, a revived Wilts & Dorset has been maintaining the nautical flavour with a bus service on the Sandbanks Ferry across Poole Harbour. For a while the plain Poppy Red livery continued to adorn the specially-adapted Bristol LH vehicles used on the ferry, as depicted by no. 3848 (YAE 520V) disembarking on the Sandbanks shore when working from Swanage to Bournemouth on the 150 route—this used to be Hants & Dorset's service 7.

Transport Milestones (3): Sudden overnight snow created havoc in the Solent area on 19 March, 1987. By mid-day the roads were clear enough to allow the National Express service 075 to depart from Southsea for London (Victoria Coach Station) as usual. This was operated by Duple-Integral 425 no. 716 of Southdown, the only example of the type in its fleet. When new it came in a silver livery with green stripes, but it was soon repainted into the standard white as seen here. At a later date the registration (C716 NYJ) was replaced by 420 DCD from a 1964-vintage convertible PD3! This futuristic coach was caught travelling at some speed heading away from Clarence Pier.

# CONCLUSION
## And Bibliography

I remember that Sixties' film, *What's it all about, Alfie* ? The past one hundred years of transport history, is a touch similar. While the teaching of history in school may be rather controversial and not always the most popular subject it is very relevant to what is going on — now, and for the future. For we live a little bit of history each day, and the understanding of it can give us a better appreciation of today — and, maybe, some answers for the future.

In Britain the Industrial Revolution generated the steam-powered railway as successor to the canals and waterways — in recent times there have been a number of special events to celebrate important anniversaries of that development; GWR 150 in 1985 and Woking 150 during 1988. In addition to these major celebrations, a culture of preservation has developed involving the retention of certain artifacts either as specific milestones along the way or just because it seemed a shame to dispose of them for scrap. An early example of inspired preservation is the 1919-vintage Thornycroft 'J' solid-tyred bus, laid aside by Portsmouth Corporation before 1930. One could argue that it is not entirely original — the body was replaced during the mid-1920s with a secondhand example (even older than the chassis) from the LGOC — and it would look better painted in the pre-1928 tramway colours as no. 10, but that is missing the point; it has been preserved, intact, for 60 years! The same Corporation retained one of its electric tramcars (no. 84), which has been restored to the original livery and is the only surviving example of a Portsmouth tram. It was very far-sighted to save a tram in 1936.

The biggest boost to private preservation owes much to that delightful Ealing comedy, *The Titfield Thunderbolt*, loosely based on the early efforts of a small band of enthusiasts to save in working order the complete Talyllyn Railway in 1951. The film featured the incredible 0-4-2 locomotive 'Lion', built in 1838 for the Liverpool & Manchester Railway and almost certainly the world's oldest working steam engine. Inspired by examples such as this, individual enthusiasts and small groups of like-minded people began to apply themselves to the difficulty of saving the status quo — preventing the wholesale scrapping of steam locomotives during the Beeching years, avoiding the ripping-up of redundant branch lines, the demolition of stations, signal cabins, goods sheds and even turn-tables. While the preservation in working order of a complete narrow gauge line like the Talyllyn was a major achievement, saving even part of a standard gauge branch was an infinitely harder task. Within the confines of the mainland area covered by this book two standard gauge lines have been saved. Passenger traffic from Corfe Castle and Swanage ceased in 1972 with the Mid-Hants line between Alton and Winchester closing the following year, but both are back in business as leisure and tourist attractions under private ownership. The magnitude of the challenge, in both instances, is a measure

*Past and present at Woolston : Against the backdrop of the new Itchen Bridge, preserved Guy Arab III no. 167 (FTR 514) stands beside one of the former floating bridges, latterly used as a night club. A modern Leyland Altlantean double-decker heads towards Southampton high above the old Woolston terminal, now disused. The Park Royal-bodied Guy is one of the oldest surviving motor buses of the former Southampton Corporation fleet.*

*Representative of one of the author's all-time favourites, Southdown's preserved 1929 Leyland Titan TD1 no. 813 (UF 4813) lines up with the only Cub coach to have survived — 1936-vintage KPZ1 no. 4 (CUF 404) — at Hambledon depot on 12 May, 1985. Since 1972 the Brush-bodied Titan has been available for occasional heritage bus services or private hire, still with its husky petrol engine. Hambledon was first served from Portsmouth by the Sussex Road Car Company in 1907, but the depot has since been sold.*

of the appeal of steam trains and country railways — and good luck to them!

What about private preservation of other forms of transport? It is not very easy to reinstate a street tramway or trolley-bus system, so even though fine vehicles exist (some fully restored) there is — as yet —nowhere to run them in the South. Few will need to be reminded of the commercial tramway which remains in operation at Blackpool and at noted museum centres such as Crich and Beamish and the best-known trolley-bus museum is at Sandtoft, near Doncaster. Other, self-propelled forms of transport are more suited to preservation by sole owners — cars, vans, fire engines, military vehicles, buses even... For this is where the man in the street — the 'man on the Clapham omnibus' — can play his modest part in saving, restoring and running a vehicle.

Perhaps I have always been a 'closet' preservationist! As a small child I can remember the end of World War II (VE Day), when Portsmouth Corporation ran the old Thornycroft around the City to celebrate victory. With its solid tyres and frail, curving staircase it looked antique — yet it was only 26 years old at the time. When I bought my Guy 'Arab' open-topper exactly three decades later, it too was 26 years old! That was in 1975, and it was obtained with redundancy pay to save it from a scrapyard fate. While it has proved to be something of a trial at times, it would have been sacrilege to have stood idly by and watched it go to the breakers. The 12v electrical system has caused no end of headaches. Trying to start 8·4 litres of diesel engine on a cold day with nothing more than a car battery is no joke, but you get used to it — and it may go some way to explaining why my son learned to drive in a Series 2 Land Rover!

Given the choice, I would have loved to preserve something even closer to my childhood memories: a Southdown 'TD1', a petrol-engined coach or a Harrington-bodied single-decker. Perhaps fate and fortune have combined to help fulfil this wish, in a way. Having founded the Vintage Transport Association in 1968, I approached Portsmouth City Museum in 1972 to arrange a joint rally for vintage vehicles — the following year the 'Southsea Spectacular' was born. While having discussions about the forthcoming event with the then Director of the Museum, Mr Barton, he happened to mention acquiring a 1935 Leyland bus from the Transport Department. None of the quartet of open-toppers that had retired at the end of the 1971 season had been disposed of at that stage — I was asked my opinion of the best one to keep, and that is how 'Titan' TD4 no. 8 (formerly 125) came to be selected. For almost a dozen years since retirement it remained out of sight, if not out of mind, before a deputation of stalwarts from the Association (ViTA) put forward an 'action plan' to bring RV 6368 back from the dead. The Museum promised to have the vehicle put into full working order again and a handful of volunteer ViTA members agreed to keep it clean, check oil levels, batteries, water etc. as necessary.

My acquaintance with RV 6368 goes back a long way: as a pupil at St. John's College between 1944 and 1948 I had occasion to catch a Corporation bus to or from Grove Road South, and with 45 possible TD4s as well as the Daimler 'utilities' plus an occasional TD2, the choice was wide. But no. 125 (RV6368) was one of those with large (6 inch) fleet number transfers at the front which appeared quite frequently on routes A and B, its 'peaked cap' shape unmistakeable even in the days when it had a roof (ie pre-1955). Journeys to school on any bus during the morning rush were a lottery, but those scheduled via Commercial Road,

*Portsmouth preserved: The old surviving Corporation tramcar (no. 84) is flanked by one of the diesel motor buses that helped to oust the tramway system in the mid-1930s, both being owned by Portsmouth City Museum. The tram has been restored to its livery of the 1920s, while Leyland Titan TD4 no. 8 (RV 6368) looks resplendent in the brighter colours that ushered in the 1930s.*

Portsmouth, were diverted via Flathouse Road, Unicorn Gate and Edinburgh Road before 9 am — and that included Corporation motor buses on service A — a practice that always seemed to compound any delays. All Corporation diesel buses, except the Daimlers, and most of the pre-war Southdowns of similar specification had a reputation amongst budding omnibologists (like me) for being ponderous in traffic, even in the days when there were only three sets of traffic lights throughout the entire City! So you can imagine my thoughts when, with the Museum's permission, I was allowed to test-drive RV 6368 (renumbered 8 during 1958) in early April 1983. Sitting in the cab, I recalled that occasion as a child at Eastney depot with no. 160: making sure it was in neutral, I switched on the ignition and pressed the starter. The engine churned over rather slowly, so the accelerator pedal was pushed to the floor and gradually each cylinder began to fire. Even with all six in action and the air thick with fumes, the engine was 'lumpy' and very sluggish to respond. With 1st gear engaged, no. 8 crept forward as I let in the clutch. Practice with some other less-antique buses enabled the crash gear-box to be mastered fairly quickly, but it was noticeable how much

earlier gear changes needed to be made with the oil so thick and heavy. After negotiating the roads out to Rudmore roundabout, the old bus had its first experience of motorways, heading north on the M275 and then west on the M27 towards Fareham (these had not been opened to traffic until 1976, five years after it had retired to the back of Eastney depot). The modest incline past Paulsgrove caused instant panic beneath the bonnet — Portsmouth, or at least the Portsmouth for which RV 6368 had been built, was flat — so I was obliged to concede 3rd gear instead of top. Then the veteran was taken aback by a sudden gust from the south-west, but the loss of revs meant plunging down into 2nd. Can you believe it? 2nd gear to heave 8.6 litres and nearly 7 tons of vintage bus up the motorway towards Fareham! Was this the famed Leyland engineering I wondered, or was RV 6368 just allergic to hills? Obliged to remain in 2nd until the summit was reached — try changing up with a crash gearbox when ascending a hill — then the old TD4 began to pick up with more enthusiasm. By the time it reached the junction for Fareham speed had risen above 30 mph and I was reluctant to rein it in, however I had no idea how much or how little fuel was swilling about in the tank. RV 6368 was pointed in the direction of the nearest garage and made it to the diesel pump without further incident. Quantities of fuel were poured in — 15 gallons, 20, 25 and more — before the beast was full. Needless to say, the gauge did not work after a lifetime's labours, but the mileometer did and there was a trip meter too. With difficulty the trip was set back to nought so that some idea of its fuel consumption might be gauged, then I attempted to restart the bus — nothing! Try as one might, every time I pushed the self-starter button there was a 'click' but no action. It was the sort of sickening sound that one dreads to hear on a cold winter morning, and which usually results in expenditure on a new battery (or in the case of a 24v bus, four 6v batteries) and it did not produce the longed-for fuming that had occurred earlier that day in Portsmouth. Sometimes on cars the starter sticks when it gets hot — could such a thing happen to a bus? The bonnet was lifted, with difficulty, to reveal not very much. With no inspiration there, as chance would have it I engaged the starting handle and turned the engine over a fraction of a revolution. Back into the cab and try again. Bingo! With a fruity roar, Leyland's pre-war pride spat fumes across the fore-court and I — at least — was delighted.

In the ensuing weeks and months nearly twelve years of inactivity were banished; oil circulated every moving part and performance improved. Now, on a good day with no passengers and a following wind, no. 8 may be expected to climb uphill on the motorway between Fareham and Portsmouth in top gear in either direction, but it can be touch and go! The veteran got rubbed-down and repainted in 'proper' colours for its Golden Jubilee in 1985, thanks to some hard work by ViTA members like Clive Wilkin, Cliff Burgess, Bob Gray and others, while Alan Pratt made a fine job of traditional hand-painting and lining-out. As

the honorary 'flagship' of Portsmouth City Museum and mascot of ViTA, it was appropriate that it should have been the official conveyance for HRH The Duchess of York when she visited Portsmouth on Tuesday, 13 June, 1989, in her capacity as Patron of Museums Year 1989; and it was great fun for me to drive it that day, a bus that had taken me to school in the City more than 40 years before.

Preservation has its ups and downs, of course. On two occasions I have broken bones when working on the TD4. My son Miles, and his friend Ian Dubber have beavered away to restore the elegant Leyland 'Tiger' that I obtained from Bournemouth in 1970; mercifully they have lost count of the hours spent rubbing-down, paint-stripping, varnishing, polishing, touching-up and generally cleaning, besides finding time to work on other preserved vehicles. Through it all has been gained a degree of satisfaction that is beyond price, aiming for the highest standard and observing with pleasure how people appreciate our transport heritage. The unselfish act of giving up a part of one's free time to further the cause of preservation can be more rewarding than mere monetary considerations — one has only to see the delight in the eyes of senior citizens when they rediscover some forgotten vehicle from their youth, or the look of wonder that can light up the faces of children who have never seen such a thing before.

It will be fascinating to look back on the 20th century, in a few years time, and we owe it to our children and our children's children to leave some examples of road and rail — as well as other kinds of transport — and their infrastructure, so that they can understand and appreciate the inheritance that has come into their hands. Today's latest creation will be tomorrow's preservation project, while "he who rides a 'Tiger' can never get off!"

## Periodicals

*Buses* ; *Buses Extra* (bi-monthly) ; *Bus Fayre* ; *Modern Tramway* ; *Railway World* ; *Modern Railways* ; *Steam Railway* ; *Steam World* ; *Railway Magazine* ; *Rail* (fort nightly) ; *BackTrack* (bi-monthly) ; *Railways South-East* (twice yearly) ; *Vintage Roadscene* (bi-monthly ; *Yesterday* ( ceased publication, back copies available from Portsmouth Publishing & Printing Ltd.).

## Buses

A.K. MacFarlane-Watt : *Southampton City Transport* ; TPC ; 1977.
Patrick Miller : *Provincial, The Gosport & Fareham Story* ; TPC ; 1981.
Alan Townsin : *75 Years of Aldershot & District* ; TPC ; 1981.
Colin Morris : *Southdown*; TPC ; 1985.
Colin Morris : *History of British Bus Services, South-East England* ; TPC ; 1980.
Colin Morris : *History of the Hants & Dorset Motor Services Ltd.* ; David & Charles ; 1973.
*The Southdown Story 1915-1965* ; Southdown Motor Services ; 1965.
Alan Lambert : *Hants & Sussex* ; A Lambert ; 1983.
Richard Newman : *Southern Vectis - The First 60 Years* ; Ensign / S.V.O.C. ; 1989.

## Tramways

S.E. Harrison : *Tramways of Portsmouth* ; LRTL ; 1955.
Portsmouth Papers : No. 45, *Portsmouth Corporation Tramways 1896-1936* ; P.C.C. ; 1986.

## General

John Horne : *Farewell to the Floating Bridges* ; Southampton City Transport & SUIAG ; 1976.
*100 Years of Southampton Transport* : S.C.T. & Southampton City Museums ; 1979.
*Portsmouth 75 Years of Transport* : City of Portsmouth Passenger Transport Dept. ; 1976.
Eric Watts : *Fares Please*; Ensign Publications ; 1987.
*Bournemouth Transport 75 Years* : Bournemouth Transport ; 1977.
*Yellow Buses 85th Anniversary 1902-1987* : Bournemouth Transport ; 1987.

## Railways

Portsmouth Papers : No. 6, *Portsmouth Railways* ; Portsmouth City Council ; 1969.
Kevin Robertson : *The Southsea Railway* ; Kingfisher Railway Productions ; 1985.
Kevin Robertson : *The Railways of Gosport* ; Kingfisher Railway Productions ; 1986.
R. Simmonds & K. Robertson : *The Bishops Waltham Branch* ; Wild Swan ; 1988.
D.L. Bradley : *LSWR Locomotives* (4 volumes) ; Wild Swan Publications ; 1985-1989.
R.A. Stone : *The Meon Valley Railway* ; Kingfisher Railway Productions ; 1983.
Gerald Daniels & L.A. Dench : *Passengers No More* ; Ian Allan ; 1973.
Robert Antell : *Southern Country Stations — LSWR* ; Ian Allan ; 1984.
Kevin Robertson : *Hampshire Railways in Old Photographs* ; Alan Sutton ; 1989.

## By the same author (D. Fereday Glenn)

*Roads, Rails & Ferries of the Solent Area, 1919-1969* ; Ian Allan ; 1980.
*Rail Routes in Hampshire & East Dorset* ; Ian Allan ; 1983.
*Bus Operators: Hants & Dorset* ; Ian Allan ; 1985.
*Rail Rover — From Kent to Cornwall* ; Alan Sutton Publishing ; 1988.
*The Last Days of Steam in Surrey and Sussex* ; Alan Sutton Publishing ; 1989.

## LP Records

*The Sounds of Bygone Transport* (TR 139) & *Southern Steam* (SPA 462) ; Argo-Transacord ( Decca Records )
*Memories of Steam* (HMA 239) ; Hallmark Records
*Johnny Morris on the Bluebell Railway* (DCM 1209) ; Discourses